Full-Time Living

Charlotte Hale Allen

Fleming H. Revell Company
Old Tappan, New Jersey

Scripture quotations identified KJV are from the King James Version of the Bible.

Old Testament Scripture quotations identified AMPLIFIED are from AMPLIFIED BIBLE, OLD TESTAMENT, copyright 1962, 1964 by Zondervan Publishing House, and are used by permission.

New Testament Scripture quotations identified AMPLIFIED are from The Amplified New Testament © The Lockman Foundation, 1954, 1958, and are used by permission.

Library of Congress Cataloging in Publication Data

Allen, Charlotte Hale.
    Full-time living.

    1. Christian life—1960–   I. Title.
BV4501.2.A423   248′.4   78-14867
ISBN 0-8007-0939-X

With thanks to God for Al and our precious five:

Rick and Carol Peper
Stan and Debbie Smith
Nancy Allen

Contents

1

The Time of Your Life

*Finding time in your life
for the things you want to do.*

Good news! There's plenty of time to do everything you want to do and feel called to do. Starting today, you can make things happen. You can begin to go *first class* in life, as God intends.

Whatever your present age, you still have time, an abundance of time, to achieve first-rate performance in the vocation (or vocations) you choose: your profession, your home life, your close personal relationships, your special ministry.

You also can find plenty of time for life's grace notes— Saturday golf games, weekend travel, or feeding the birds and the roses. You might take up fast tennis games or leisurely picnics; enjoy heavy reading or light laughter; make time for singing, sending valentines, or creative goofing off.

How? I call the method *full-time living,* which simply describes your decision to *live* those sixteen to eighteen waking hours each day instead of playing them by rote.

But you're already living full-time; you hate to think it

might get any fuller. You're like the lady who exclaimed to Dr. Paul L. Walker, our pastor, "This abundant life is about to kill me!"

I relate to her and suspect you do, too. After all, how many men and women can you name who seem truly liberated from the tyranny of time pressures? I just counted and can't even come up with five. Nevertheless, I'd like to challenge you:

- Suppose you could enjoy at least twice as much living as you now get for the 168 hours per week you spend on life. Would you take it?
- And what if you began adventuring toward the greatest thrill of your life thus far, even before you finish reading this book. Do you believe that's possible?

It is. I *know* it is, because two years ago I learned how to turn my own mostly happy and productive life into something much more forceful and satisfying.

At that time, my horizons literally exploded outward so that today I do twice as many of the things I really want to do as I ever managed to do before—with half the tension and twice the joy. Better still, I'll probably double that again in the next twelve months.

Since then, dozens of men and women in my seminars, plus numerous other successful, achieving, and unusually happy individuals I've interviewed—some well known, others little known—have convinced me it's possible for anyone to exchange the half-life most of us accept for the sort of full-time living few people ever experience.

You can learn how. You can begin today.

This book will show you some practical, logical means by

which you can identify God's present call on your life. You'll also learn some ways to recognize God's particular purpose for *you*. And from there, you'll see how to find your vocation(s) and establish His priorities for this day.

You're about to begin a fascinating voyage, with your individual life trip entirely unlike that of any other passenger in the world. Your ticket, of course, includes the full set of new goals you'll give yourself—and what a bonus they are! Goals guarantee you surprising and immediate joy, as well as long-term pleasure and profit.

And then we approach our destination—successful time management. Yes, you *will* get there. What's more, getting there is half the fun!

How do I know? Because I'm making the trip, a two-year voyage for me so far. And the going is great, though I admit I only signed on out of desperation.

You see, I'd worked out a good life-style for myself during five years of single piggishness. In retrospect, those years represent an almost idyllic period of peace and order, a time when I could absolutely wallow in silence anytime I wished. It was a season for working all night whenever I wanted, or listening to an entire Brahms symphony uninterrupted. During those years very few fingerprints appeared on the woodwork.

And then came Al. Incredibly enough, during the lull before the marriage, I gave absolutely no thought to the impact an Al might have on my schedule. By then, of course, The Schedule was going tickety-tock; there seemed no reason to think it might miss a beat.

If two hearts beat as one, I reasoned, shouldn't our lives synchronize equally well? And if Al could understand the demands of periodic book deadlines, couldn't I become flexible about the occasional work overloads in his profession?

Theoretically, yes. In practice, however, neither business trips nor book deadlines tripped us up, but just the fact that loving another person requires a significant amount of time. What's more, you can't really schedule it.

Who'd ever plan on an emergency midnight ride to the farmers' market for a bushel of really ripe peaches or a mammoth striped watermelon?

How could I imagine that something six foot three, who whistles first thing in the morning, hangs towels up crooked, and eagerly anticipates Monday-night football, would fit neatly into the empty space in my simple life?

No way. At least, not neatly. The Bible clearly instructs wives to adapt themselves to their husbands, and I intended to adapt graciously. I learned to smile at the shock of tennis shoes parked beside the sofa and pretended not to mind whenever work—his or mine—threw us a curve.

Life, meanwhile, provided blessing after blessing for us. Six weeks after Al and I married, my son Stan married Debbie, his demure young redhead. A year later, Carol, Al's older daughter, brought a young lawyer named Rick into our circle. Then Nancy, who reminds me so much of Al, moved to Atlanta to live near her daddy and me.

Thus in just two years I found myself not only loving Stan, but Carol and Nancy as well, plus a wonderful new son and daughter by marriage. Suddenly we had five super young men and women from age twenty-three down to eighteen. True, they were full-grown and beautifully self-sufficient, but loving them still took time!

Al and I thrived on the long-distance phone calls that recorded so many milestones. "Daddy, I *know* I flunked

that biology exam. Yes, I'm sure. I might not even make a
B . . . ."

"Mom and Al, I want you to know I'm going to be or-
dained next Sunday."

"Daddy! Rick passed the bar exam!"

"Hey, you guys, I got the job . . . ."

God showered Al and me with blessings, and we accepted His goodness with amazement and gratitude. We
thanked Him for precious new friends, new social outlets,
some business honors. He gave us a new house (actually it
was twenty years old) that needed new wallpaper and paint
and plumbing. Al sang in the Sanctuary Choir; we became
active in our church's singles' ministry; we started accepting invitations to speak in churches and in Christian meetings. Also, and this may have been the final straw, Al gave
me the Siamese kitten I'd wanted all my life—the inimi-
table Amy.

Fantastic! Approaching age fifty, Al and I thanked God
with all our hearts for His abundant blessings on our lives.
Again and again we told Him, and told everyone else, that
we'd never been so happy, nor had we dreamed life could
be so good.

Despite these truths, however, some other disturbing
and much less pleasant truths began to appear. Quite simply, I never could seem to make life come out even. I'd
always prided myself on my disciplined life-style, but that
began to disappear, despite my determined and almost
heroic efforts toward self-control.

No matter how carefully I scheduled things, unexpected
house guests or church meetings, and very often extra
cooking and housework, seemed to mushroom at the worst
possible times. First my professional work, and soon even

my prayer life, began to happen only by fits and starts.

Unfortunately, Al couldn't seem to help me with my problems. If I tried to analyze with him the causes of what by now I saw as a chaotic household, he'd simply pat me on the shoulder and tell me to hang loose. "Don't be so hard on yourself," he'd say encouragingly. "After all, do I complain? Everything will be okay."

It got less and less okay from my point of view. What's more, my increasing moodiness and spells of short temper—always fierce and unpredictable and terribly embarrassing to me—couldn't be dismissed with the phrase "losing the victory." I began to fear that though I'd gained the whole world I still might lose the victory permanently—right in my own house.

As my practical problems increased, my joy decreased. I began to seek God continuously, mystified that I couldn't seem to get a good grip on the happiness He wanted us to enjoy. Did I pray or did I complain? Probably both. But when I consulted the Bible and my concordance for references concerning time, I was astonished at how little I found. In Ephesians 5:15–17 (KJV) the apostle Paul admonished:

> See then that ye walk circumspectly, not as
> fools, but as wise, Redeeming the time, because
> the days are evil. Wherefore be ye not unwise, but
> understanding what the will of the Lord is.

Surely, I thought in real frustration, I want to use my time wisely and know the will of God for my life. But how? And when I listed my priorities—first my relationship to God, then to my husband, our children and home life,

Christian fellowship and service, my Christian writing—all seemed in order.

"It's ironic that I always seemed to have very little trouble with time management before I met Jesus," I told Al one evening. "I always had so much energy, such enthusiasm, I guess my life pretty well fell into place. I felt competent.

"Since Jesus, though, my values have changed. My problem is, I know God expects me to be a good wife and mother. Surely He expects me to run this house really well. But then, with church and friends and everything else, what do I do about my writing?

"It's really not a part-time job," I said defensively, "and I still think I'm called to do it. If the house looks decent, I've skimped on writing; if I write all day, nothing else gets done. And I'm sick of complaining!"

"You need some help," Al observed.

"I can't help but believe God is trying to teach me to manage *without* help," I said hopelessly.

"In that case, what one thing robs you of the most time? What's your biggest block?" Al asked in his most reasonable tone of voice.

"People!"

"What do you mean?"

"I mean ordinary friends and phone calls and children who want to know how to write a job résumé. Every night we ask God to give us someone tomorrow who needs to hear about Jesus, and every day someone shows up. That takes time.

"What about the neighbor who locks herself out of her house and comes to me? How about that divorcée you thought I could help? And why do people think of us if they happen to get drunk and suicidal?

"Honey, we pray to be useful to the Kingdom. We care. We want to serve. I don't want to cut things out of our lives, but learn how to add things in. But it's all so unpredictable and unwieldy, and I feel like I'm losing.

"How do the other saints manage to cope? Where do they find enough time?"

I decided, with Al's help, to seek the Lord for some real answers and to persevere until those answers appeared. He and I worked together on household schedules, experimented endlessly on ways to put it all together. I read everything I could find on effective time usage and interviewed anyone who might offer new insights.

Some weeks flowed so smoothly that it seemed we might be getting somewhere. Other times we bogged down. I could identify strongly with the psalmist David's cry:

> Lord, make me to know mine end, and the
> measure of my days, what it is; that I may know
> how frail I am. Behold, thou hast made my days
> as an handbreadth; and mine age is as nothing
> before thee: verily every man at his best state is
> altogether vanity.
>
> Psalms 39:4, 5 KJV

Eventually though, I came to see that many of the strongest Christians I know remain continually oppressed by clocks, calendars, and staff meetings. It's astonishing to realize that hectic, frantic days, odd travel schedules, peculiar eating habits, and subsequent periods of emotional depression often are as commonplace to the achieving

Christian as to his secular brother.

It did not reassure me to learn that very few King's kids claim to have much of a grip on that peace that passes understanding or to know in any real way that His yoke is easy and His burden is light. But we all talk a good game sometimes, and even as one would confess to me that he really didn't handle his own time and life any too well, he'd nevertheless offer a scriptural prescription for what ailed me. "God promises to lengthen the days of His righteous," one man assured me.

"Just how does that work for you?"

"Well, ah, actually it helps to have a good secretary," he explained somewhat lamely. And we both laughed.

That was *then*. Somewhat later, however, as our pastor would say, "The Bible came crashing through." It was all in the Bible, of course, as you knew it would be—only not filed under *time*, but *life*.

Of course! Jesus had outlined my own situation—and that of every man in the world—when He said: "The thief cometh not, but for to steal, and to kill, and to destroy: I am come that they might have life, and that they might have it more abundantly" (John 10:10 KJV).

I've been robbed every day of my life, and so have you. We're used to grand larceny and the dedicated, professional ripping off of our most irreplaceable treasures: our dreams and deep desires, new experiences, love and intimacy, any hope and expectation of significant personal growth and achievement.

God allowed me to realize, in vivid and specific detail, exactly how much stealing, killing, and destruction I had acceded to in my own experience. Where time was concerned, I could see, I literally had become penny wise and

pound foolish. I quibbled over fifteen minutes here and
half a morning there, while God's grand plan for my life
year by year got postponed.

When you're dismayed by the facts of too much struggle
and not enough payoff, too many duties and too few joys,
there's only one place to go—to the One who always cares.
God's answer to me came in the form of a surprising question: "Wilt thou be healed?"

Yes, it required much inner healing. God had to show
me why I required such tight control over my cir-
cumstances. He had to reveal my carefully covered-over
fears, then gently focus the searchlight of the Holy Spirit
on sins of pride and self-sufficiency, the inability to accept
help.

But what has all that to do with my obsession about time
management? And how could it possibly help your
crowded situation?

Simply, what worked for me will work for you. And
full-time living *does* work—especially for those of us who
often feel desperately hemmed in by the demands of
household, school, or office routine, plus the inexorable
pressures of endlessly trying to meet other people's needs
and expectations.

Full-time living literally changed my life overnight, and
I've seen it transform other lives just as speedily. The process is simple enough, but not necessarily easy. It has required hard work, tough self-examination, and, in my
case, a decision to quit kidding myself about the real facts
of my own life. Full-time living requires a genuine willingness to quit making excuses. It also demands a full-time
willingness to *change*—and change hurts!

Today, however, payoff time has arrived. Both my family and my calendar attest to some pretty dramatic results around here. Never before have my weeks been more crowded or my days longer—nor have I ever been more absorbed in reality. For the first time in my life, I know how to handle real challenges without undue stress and pressure. I've learned to invest the time and energy savings in interesting new ventures.

The first such investment popped up exactly two months after God introduced me to my new way of life. By that time my friends had become curious as to what had caused such radical changes in my habits and personality. I seemed unnaturally happy and vigorous and couldn't seem to explain exactly what had caused it. "Maybe you'll write a book," they'd say, and that sounded like a good idea. I began to collect notes and clippings for my file labeled THE TIME OF YOUR LIFE.

One January morning, as I explored with myself the possibility of a book-to-be, I heard myself say aloud: "I'd like to give a seminar entitled 'The Time of Your Life.'"

Incredible! How could a woman who refused even to teach Sunday school, who never spoke before groups, who was terrified to second the motion at a P.T.A. meeting, lead a seminar?

"That's *crazy*. You can't do anything like that," I rebuked myself.

"I certainly can if I want to!" I shot back defiantly, and that ended all further conversation with myself for that day. I was too scared to speak to myself again.

By the next week, following much argument with the Lord, I'd begun to outline the material. I wondered what I'd do with it once it was finished, since normally I don't run all over Atlanta offering to teach untried and unproven material to unknown audiences. At least, I thought I didn't.

Perhaps you've guessed by now that God opened the door for my first seminar in His own way, with absolutely no help from me. From that first unbelievably joyous experience (incidentally, totally free from fear!) many subsequent opportunities arose.

I'll share with you in this book many of the inspiring and exciting things God did for people in the "Time of Your Life" seminars. How much their insights, their Spirit-controlled thinking, enriches my own experience with the Lord!

Together we laugh, cry, pray, and challenge one another. Again and again we see how much Jesus longs to occupy every life, not only filling it to overflowing with love, peace, and joy, but also providing opportunities beyond number.

He wants to offer *you* full-time living today. Let's begin now:

My objective is: to discover my vocation(s), learn how to establish goals, choose priorities skillfully, and begin to do the things that really matter.

I shall learn how to *make things happen.* This means taking dominion over my own life, as God instructs me, and tossing out trivia and trash:

to make room for more love, more friends, and new experiences;

to solidify existing relationships;

to expand into new ones;

and to allow God to begin a new work—

    on myself,

    my environment,
    in my church,
    my job,
    my neighborhood,
    my family.
And in the process, I shall come into full-time living—
Christ's abundant life!

"That sounds just great," I hear you saying, "but how
can I ever do all that?"

The first step of our journey starts with *you*—who you
are, and where you are. Let's go!

2

Your Springboard

*You can begin to take dominion
over your life.*

Today is the springboard to where you'll land and what you'll be doing five years from now. Where are you headed? Where do you want to go?

"Wherever God puts me," I used to say in a totally sincere but unthinking way. "Surely He can tell me what He wants me to do."

That's a common attitude among Christians, for many wonderful children of God fail to realize *He has given us dominion over our own lives.*

What a shock to perceive that God holds me accountable not only for the way I live my life, but also for the way I plan or fail to plan exactly what I hope that life will contain. As the Bible says, "A man's mind plans his way, but the Lord directs his steps and makes them sure" (Proverbs 16:9 AMPLIFIED).

"How do I know where my life's going, or even where I want it to go?" asked a young woman named June. "It all depends upon my husband: his job, his income, his weekend plans, even his diet. My life is just tacked on to his, and that will never change."

Bob, a divorced father in his early forties, had a similar outlook. "I always wrapped myself up in my family and lived in light of their plans. In fact, though I've always been fascinated by nature photography—I used to sell my color shots to national magazines—I felt so guilty about spending time away from the kids that I let dust accumulate in my darkroom.

"I never spent much money on myself and didn't develop any personal interests. Now I feel socially backward and out of it. I'm beginning to think I should have been more selfish all those years.

"How in the world can I figure out where I'm headed? I have no idea of what I really want, much less where I'm going, at this point in my life."

And then there's Mary Elizabeth, well married and proud of her five outstanding sons and daughters. "I wouldn't trade my life for all the tea in China. I've been blessed!" she declared. "Of course, six years from now the nest will be empty. It scares me to think about it; sometimes I wonder what will happen to me then. Not often, though. Maybe Tom and I will travel, and then the grandchildren will come along . . . ."

When you invest an evening in taking inventory, you'll begin immediately to identify what you want in life. It's hard work, actually—surprisingly hard. But I promise you it will produce results. The moment you begin to research that mostly unknown and virtually unexplored continent that is your Self, you embark on a winning streak.

It worked that way for me and seems to pay off for everyone else I know who really tries it. We'll share some of those "springboard stories" throughout this book, but right now, let's look at you.

To do the job right, you'll need several sheets of paper, pen or pencils, a comfortable chair, and perhaps a cup of coffee. Pick a time when you're likely not to be disturbed, since it's best to do each of these exercises in succession.

We're going to use a stream-of-consciousness technique that's become a favorite in executive planning seminars. Perhaps you've encountered it before, but if so, no matter; just go at it again. It's fun, after all, and we're going to add a few new twists to an old standby.

At the top of your paper write: WHAT I WANT IN MY LIFE. Below that write: DURING MY LIFETIME.

Now take *two minutes* to list your lifetime goals and desires. Write as rapidly as possible without stopping to think. Don't censor yourself or be too discriminating; just jot down absolutely anything that comes to mind, no matter how trivial, overly ambitious, or impossible it seems.

Stop after two minutes. Reread your list to see if you'd like to add anything important.

Title your next page DURING THE NEXT FIVE YEARS. Take two minutes to list everything you'd like to do, learn, or acquire during the next five years. Remember, the sky's the limit. Let your imagination rip. Have fun thinking up outrageous desires!

After two minutes, check this list briefly for any important omissions and add them now.

Your third page really gets down to business. Title this one IF I HAD ONLY SIX MONTHS TO LIVE. Imagine that you know you'll have only six months remaining in your lifespan. In two minutes, list everything you'd include in those months. Make them the best six months of your entire life. As before, read your list and make any significant additions you like.

Now comes the part that's really fun. Starting with quiz number one, carefully choose your top three priority items, numbering them according to importance. Do the same for part two and part three. Survey your choices carefully, but take no more than five or six minutes for this.

What did you discover?

If your top three priority items on each list happened to coincide, you're a rare bird—you know pretty well what you want. That doesn't happen too often.

If you encounter some wild discrepancies between priorities on the three lists, it's fascinating to ask yourself why. And if you found it almost impossible to think of anything at all you really want—during your lifetime, five years hence, or even next week—that tells you something important too.

Personally, I got stuck almost at once; I couldn't seem to play the game. Why? Because I really didn't have many desires of my own. Remember, I was going to "do what God wanted," and whatever fit in with the rest of my family—as if I had no further responsibility.

Many, if not most, of the women and quite a few of the men I encounter seem to fall into that same trap. In fact, if you ask the next dozen people you meet where they think they'll be five years from now, probably all twelve will say they have no idea.

By now, you are one of the exceptions. You have identified—even by this crude means—some of your own important values. Probably you are surprised at some of what emerged; maybe some ideas excited you.

"All three of my lists say I want to earn money," one woman said, shocked. She looked as though she disapproved of herself for having any interest whatever in money.

"What does that mean to you?" someone in the class asked.

"Well, I had no idea I was materialistic," she said defensively. "If I hadn't done these lists I guess I never would have known it."

She had to realize there's no right or wrong to what's itemized, and no need to feel that her desire for money necessarily is materialistic, grasping, or "not nice."

Indeed, many Christians discover that full-time living will require them to become fully responsible for managing money well. As their objectives and purposes emerge, they see a clear need for mature stewardship of both time and money. Many of us begin to see that our own immature attitudes toward finances can prevent God from fulfilling His plans for us.

Others of us, as we survey our three lists, note with dismay that our desires don't reflect the lives we're actually spending right now.

You'd like to sell real estate when the children leave home? What are you doing about it today?

You'd like to begin to turn over more of your business to others so you can travel and testify to Christian groups? What can you do about that today?

You'd like to open your home for a weekly Bible study? Who would teach? Should you enroll in a Bible school today?

But perhaps your three lists turned out discouragingly vague and inconclusive. You're really confused as to what you *do* want, or you have the disappointing feeling that you "flunked." Don't stop here! This next—and final—

exam is for each one of us, but especially for you.

Please take another sheet of paper and title it MY PER-
SONAL APTITUDE TEST.

Now list every childhood dream and ambition you can
recall, no matter how naive or silly it seems from today's
perspective. Take five minutes for this.

Review your paper in case there's something you wish to
add. Now, place a star beside every childhood dream that
came true. Place a check beside every childhood dream you
still wish *might come true*.

Were those checked items on any of your three earlier
lists? Are they still valid for you?

This final part of your personal analysis might offer the
deepest insights of all; often that happens. The reason? As
Dr. Glenn Clark wrote, "When God created an acorn, He
intended to make an oak tree." Accordingly, our childhood dreams and desires often reveal with startling clarity
those fundamental talents and personality traits placed
within us by God Himself when He formed our natures.

In "The Time of Your Life" seminars, this part of our
sharing can have very funny or triumphant or poignant
results.

"I wanted to be a nun," one lady recalled in a surprised
voice, "but I married and had five sons."

"I wanted to be a convict and wear a striped suit," a
businessman said. "Then I changed to a cowboy, because I
liked the boots and hat. After that I dreamed of becoming a helicopter pilot—and that came true. Today I want to
live a Spirit-filled life and give every part of myself to
Christ.

"I can see that from the beginning of my life I've
always wanted adventure. I wanted something far out

of the ordinary—and I found it!"

Often these childhood reminiscences are light-hearted—such as that of the charming blond who had wanted nothing else but to grow up and be Liza Minelli—but occasionally they're profound. Tears streamed down one woman's face as she listed her childhood hopes. We were sharing around the circle, but she cried so hard she couldn't see to read.

"You don't have to read your list unless you want to," I began, but she shook her head positively and insisted she must read her paper to us.

When at last she composed herself and began to read in a shaky voice, every other person in the room wept too. The child this gentle woman had been wanted a kind and loving father, enough food and clothes, a happy mother who didn't have to work, a warm and loving home, and so on. It was a long and heartbreaking list. She ended with this statement: "Even before I knew God, He knew the desires of my heart and wanted to provide everything I wanted and needed.

"He is the tender, loving Father I longed for, and He never will reject me. I want you all to know that everything I wanted as a child has come true, but if I hadn't made this list, I wouldn't have realized it!"

It's a good idea to date your four worksheets and keep them. When you do the first three pages again in a month or so, you'll hardly recognize yourself. And why should you? What you did today, after all, is a springboard to *then*.

By now you've begun to gain some ideas of what you hope you'll see come to fruition during the rest of your life. Perhaps the lists made you feel slightly uncomfortable, or perhaps you saw them as a somewhat selfish exercise. "The Christian always should live his life for other people," one man chided. "His own life should not be important to him."

The person who really wants to live for others, of course, needs a whole and healthy Self from which to give. The Bible tells us that God created us only a little lower than the angels, that He knows when a sparrow falls, that He has numbered the very hairs of our heads. Psalms 139:2, 3 (KJV) says, "Thou knowest my downsitting and mine uprising, thou understandest my thought afar off. Thou compassest my path and my lying down, and art acquainted with all my ways."

Every page of the Bible attests to God's desire for an intimate involvement with your life. He founded your life, and you can be sure He wants to see it bring forth beautiful fruit.

Psalms 37:4–6 (KJV) promises:

> Delight thyself also in the Lord; and he shall give thee the desires of thine heart. Commit thy way unto the Lord; trust also in him; and he shall bring it to pass. And he shall bring forth thy righteousness as the light, and thy judgment as the noonday.

Commit those pages you just wrote to the Lord. They are your first step toward full-time living. Offer them to Him and expect Him to give you the desires of your heart.

After all, who placed those desires there in the beginning?

3

Good News—Now!

*Today is the most important day
in your life.*

There's unlimited potential in your life today. *This* day. Now that you're on your way toward full-time living, you know that. But how do you get started?

You start now. Jesus Christ demonstrated the dynamics of living in the present; He showed us an imperishable example of taking things as they come, not fretting over the past or worrying about the future. ". . . Sufficient unto the day is the evil thereof," He said (Matthew 6:34 KJV).

Think of Jesus, His way of entering into each situation as it arrived, teaching His disciples, visiting friends, caressing children, calming the storm. The Bible doesn't tell us He lived by anxiety or procrastination. He lived not only by the day, but by the hour!

When we learn the importance of *now*, we discover a lot of new power. Not only did Jesus understand that power principle, but psychologists advocate it too. The renowned William James said, "Seek the first possible opportunity to act on every good resolution you make." Other experts agree that procrastination tends to paralyze the will, while prudent action serves as a catalyst.

You literally cannot overestimate the importance of *now* in your life. Full-time living begins for you at precisely this point.

The best way you can prove that to yourself is to take stock of your *now*—especially if you believe you know in dismal detail exactly where you are. For example, I might tell you that I must complete this book in the next two weeks, that Al and I will fulfill speaking dates out of town this month, plan having dinner guests, possibly helping Nancy move to a new apartment, and Amy's presenting us with her first kittens.

That's not enough, however. You need to give yourself much more solid information from which to plan your journey. It's time to delineate the facts of your present life-style and discover the dynamics of *now*.

Once again, find pen and paper and make yourself comfortable. It's good to date these papers, which you will title PRESENT LIFE PROFILE.

First, place a minutes-per-week or hours-per-week estimate beside each category listed here. Write in other major occupations which apply to your life, with time estimates. (These estimates are necessarily rough, since some categories overlap.)

Housecleaning	Errands
Office work	Cooking
Commuting	Paying bills
Child care	Husband's needs
Car pools	Wife's needs

Yard work	Neighbors
Household repairs	Relating to children
Shopping	Relating to spouse
Wardrobe maintenance	Letter writing
Entertaining	Telephoning
Committee work	Lunching with friends
Church work	Television
Prayer	Gardening
Bible study	Handicrafts
Dating	Community projects
Personal grooming	Education
Exercise	Wasting time
Naps or rest	Relating to parents
Hobbies	Volunteer work
Christian fellowship	Other

Once you conscientiously compute that list, it may reveal you're occupied more than the 168 hours a week contains. What to do?

Phase two of your Present Life Profile helps you analyze the figures and reveals what's actually going on. Ask yourself these questions:

1. How many hours per week do I sleep?

2. How many waking hours am I occupied in an average week?

3. How many hours of discretionary time do I have per week?

4. How many hours do I need?

Place a check mark beside any activity listed which you're not doing but would like to do. Place a cross mark beside any activity you're doing but would love to quit!

5. How many hours per week would I need in order to

accomplish those items I checked? (Be as realistic as possible.)

6. How many hours per week would I save if I could stop doing those things I crossed off my list?

Now take a long look at your totals. Do you like what you see? Perhaps you can see glaring instances of time abuse, obvious places you can find that free time you so desperately need. If so, praise the Lord!

More likely, however, you see you need hours that are made of elastic. You're doing too much, and there's no way to cut down. If so, you praise the Lord too!

When you survey the number of hours—staggering, sometimes!—God allows you to fulfill, it can change your perspective from one of frustration and self-criticism to that of gratitude and submission.

Some periods of our lives—particularly those that deal with the full-time rearing of children or the devoted care of ill or elderly relatives—simply can't be made efficient. In fact, efficiency is not the aim. The apostle Paul instructs us so well at times like that: "Make love your aim." And again, "His grace is sufficient for me."

Others of us, however, certainly can improve the status quo. If that's your case, now is the time to decide. It's a good idea to write a little contract with yourself:

I Have Decided to Try

1. To stop:

2. To begin:

_____   _____
  (Date)   (Signature)

One man figured feverishly, with furrowed brow and chewed-on pencil, only to announce dramatically, "God just showed me He wants to deliver me from all yard work!"

He was kidding, though. As he explained to his laughing colleagues, "I'm delighted to realize how many hours I'm working outdoors. It's good for the yard and sure beats paying to exercise at a health spa!"

A mother figured out that she was spending a total of two workdays a week washing, drying, and folding clothes. When she decided to make her three young daughters responsible for their own laundry, she learned, to her consternation, that they considered her a "bad mommy" for expecting them to take over the chores.

"That really concerned me," she told us. "Obviously they need the character training even more than I need the time I'm saving as a result of my analysis."

Another mother, disheartened at the time consumed by long daily drives to and from school with her teenage son, discovered that they could pray together and read the Bible aloud as one or the other drove. "Mark loves it; it has become such a precious time for both of us," Bette said. "And to think I used to resent those trips!"

Most of us who calculate our Present Life Profile honestly find a few time leaks we can eliminate. However, when we release ourselves from any task, large or small, it's always best to know exactly what we want to place in that time. If we don't plan ahead, the time slot will be filled anyhow, often with negligible results.

Bob decided he would cut down on his television time by 50 percent and spend his savings on a vigorous prayer campaign. That necessitated his changing many habits, however, because he'd been accustomed to dozing in front of the television set until bedtime each evening.

Bob decided he would begin going to bed at ten each evening, forgo all late TV shows, and rise two hours earlier every morning for a quiet time with the Lord. "Needless to say, this decision transformed my life," he confessed. "The day starts off right when I seek the Lord first thing in the morning. I have time to pray for each member of my family, the guys I work with, and other people God puts on my mind.

"I'm seeing mind-blowing miracles these days. The best one, for sure, is the way He's increasing love and patience in *me!*"

Occasionally a time tally reveals that a man or woman has created a badly lopsided schedule due to excessive telephoning, visiting, reading, and the like. Immediately we must suspect that we're attempting to escape some unpleasant situation in our lives, and we must seek God for His wisdom.

Virtually all of us are escapists to some extent. It's simply a question of when and where we choose to goof off and how much it costs us or others.

But the woman who sleeps in every morning and can't find the energy to do her housework, or the man who slumps in front of the tube every night of the week and refuses to join the rest of the family, needs to be encouraged to seek professional counseling.

If you're in that category, you possibly suffer from clinical depression—which some doctors name as America's most predominant illness. You'll want to consult your family physician or your pastor for advice on where to go for help in achieving the full-time living you need and deserve.

But for the rest of us, the typically half-disciplined or nondirected types, there's a real high ahead when we learn the importance of *now*.

Let's begin this minute. What shall we decide to give ourselves first—tennis lessons or Bible class? Could I possibly rearrange the car pool? Or if not, is there another way to redeem the time?

The good news is *now*. The past is forgiven, the future unknown. Now is the hour when you and I can experience the full-time living God promises throughout His Word.

As we wait on Him, it helps to memorize those Scriptures which fill this moment with power. One I like is 1 Thessalonians 5:16–18 (KJV):

> Rejoice evermore. Pray without ceasing. In every thing give thanks: for this is the will of God in Christ Jesus concerning you.

That's the good news—NOW!

4

Your Purpose

What is your mission in life?

What is the great purpose for which you were created? What is your special mission in this life? And how much does God treasure *your* particular Self?

At times we linger beside a crib, looking down on a sleeping baby, awed at the potential within that tiny but already determined person. What will you become? we wonder.

Picture Jesus standing beside us asking that same crucial question. He knows our Father's purpose for each life; He knows the divine plan for me, but have I yet asked Him what that might be? Has it even occurred to me to ask?

I must know *God's* purpose for my life before I can make much sense out of living. Again and again the Bible reiterates that fact. As Paul wrote to the Philippians:

> . . . but this one thing I do, forgetting those things which are behind, and reaching forth unto those things which are before, I press toward the mark for the prize of the high calling of God in Christ Jesus.
>
> Philippians 3:13, 14 KJV

It's a thrill even to imagine the possibilities within my
high calling of God in Christ Jesus! Paul tells us that
". . . as many as are led by the Spirit of God, they are the
sons of God" and that we've ". . . received the spirit of
adoption, whereby we cry, Abba, Father" (Romans 8:14,
15 KJV).

And if that weren't riches enough, Paul also assures us
that if we're children, we're also heirs of God and joint
heirs with Christ (Romans 8:17), which plainly shows that
our heavenly Father had no small plans for us when He
brought us into existence.

What, then, are my great plans for myself? How do they
line up with God's purpose for my life? And why do so few
of us have any inkling of what His special call on our lives
might be?

I believe most of us don't work hard enough to find
answers to those questions. Too often we merely hope for
a *good* life instead of seeking to live a *great* life.

Mark Twain wrote, "God has put something noble and
good into every heart His hand created." Not only that,
but God so prizes each man and woman He creates that He
chooses to lead us *personally* to eternal salvation. What's
more, the Bible tells us He is concerned with every detail
of our lives.

God cares. He does not delegate the tasks concerning us,
but cares for us Himself. The Bible says God created us to
do great exploits; He has infinite faith in each life He
created.

You surely have seen lives miraculously transformed
when turned over in their totality to Jesus Christ. Incredible changes occur, sometimes apparently overnight, as the

imperfect human personality begins to be re-created into the image of our Lord.

The individual who finds God's highest purpose for his existence discovers another dimension of vital experience as his life comes into true focus. Although he still sees "through a glass darkly," as Paul wrote, his otherwise mundane life now becomes illuminated by the One who is the Light of the world.

You need to live in that Light. You want to find your specific high calling in Christ Jesus.

But how?

Recently our "Time of Your Life" class accepted that same challenge. We decided to seek God each day for one full month with one objective in mind—that He would reveal to each person His divine plan for that life.

We agreed we wouldn't tell God what we thought that might be, but really would practice trying to listen to His voice during regularly scheduled quiet times with Him. We claimed Jeremiah 33:3, which someone has termed "God's telephone number." Here God speaks through His prophet, saying: "Call unto me, and I will answer thee, and shew thee great and mighty things, which thou knowest not" (KJV).

Our class included babes in Christ as well as longtime prayer warriors. None of us had many preconceived notions of what God might do, but we entered into our spiritual experiment with high hopes and expectations. God, of course, did not disappoint us.

The authority for our decision came from Jesus Christ in Matthew 7:7, 8 (KJV). We decided to take Jesus' instructions literally:

Ask, and it shall be given you; seek, and ye shall
find; knock, and it shall be opened unto you: For
every one that asketh receiveth; and he that
seeketh findeth; and to him that knocketh it shall
be opened.

Phillips Brooks said, "It does not take great men to do
great things; it only takes consecrated men." Our prayer
experimenters consecrated themselves to the task of hearing from God, and one by one they reported that His
purpose for them was a lot larger than they could have
thought up themselves.

"The ideas that blew across my mind each day never
could have come out of my own head," one man told me.
"I simply don't think on such large-scale terms."

Several of us discovered that God's apparent purpose
for us was something quite akin to our professions, but
several dimensions beyond anything we'd ever before en-
visioned. It intrigued us to see just how limited our thinking had been and how much God wanted to stretch and
expand the minds that sought Him even briefly.

For example, Virginia Proctor was surprised to discover
the Lord wants her to build houses! "At first it took a while
to put it all together," she reported, "but, after praying it
through, it seems to make perfect sense to me."

Virginia had been a real-estate broker in North Carolina
for several years before moving to Georgia and retiring to
rear her children fulltime. However, during the recent
economic recession, the building industry in our area was
hit disastrously hard. Ray, Virginia's architect husband,
was one of many in his profession who were financially
"knocked down" for a spell.

"It made sense for me to return to real-estate work while

Ray and I got back on our feet," Virginia said. "But I was dragging *my* feet. I just didn't seem to have the pep and initiative I once had; the real enthusiasm for listing and selling houses was missing. Though I prayed about it, I couldn't see why.

"At that point we entered 'The Time of Your Life.' Ray and I did the prayer experiment with everyone else, and the Lord showed me that Ray and I will be building houses for people to make their homes in. These homes will be in a low-average price range. The Lord showed me what the price would be and what sort of profit He expects us to make and what we'll give to His Kingdom.

"I feel Ray will help me greatly with this, but it will be my work and not his; I believe God has special work for Ray."

As Virginia and Ray prayed each day about these ideas, the couple realized that God was placing thoughts in their minds in an extraordinarily orderly and thorough fashion. "We saw, for example, that we'd not begin any actual building for three to five years," Virginia said. "At first we thought that was due to our monetary stress, but God showed me we'd be able to get the money we'll need for this purpose. The delay is for my training.

"I see I must get out and learn what makes a subdivision sell. The best way to do that is to learn why people in this area choose the houses they buy. That means I must do my homework—get in my car and work at finding the right house for my client."

Her spiritual gift of discernment helps Virginia sell houses, she believes. "When I walk into a house, I can instantly tell you if I could sell it," she told me. "You feel ease and peace and happiness in some houses, while others represent turmoil; you don't want to stay there.

"At times I know instantly that I've entered a Christian home; other times I say this is a divorce situation, and I'm right. As I prayed about the ideas God was putting in my mind, I realized that I could put the right kind of 'feeling' into the Christian homes—maybe even Christian villages—we'll build."

During the month-long prayer experiment, our class began talking about goals. "Things started becoming concrete about building," Virginia related. "I began to see the number of houses we'd build and the amount of money we'd need. The Lord showed me He could guide me in these practical ways, but He cautioned me, too; I must never change my life-style so much that I'd become too busy to listen to my friends and pray with them.

"The one big question I had about this project was, could we build a quality home and still make money in this price range? My architect husband feels that we can.

"He and I began inspecting subdivision houses during our prayer month. Ray could see you could spend a few dollars more and make much better homes. The Lord doesn't do things halfway!"

Finding God's purpose for my life helps me transcend the mundane activities of today. It's exciting to see how simple events come together to work out His patterns.

C. Linden Sledge, a San Antonio banker, learned this soon after he committed his life to Christ several years ago. "He revolutionized my life," Corky Sledge said, "yet my goals didn't change that much; it's just that the emphasis strengthened.

"I found that my values already lined up pretty well with those in the Scriptures, so in a sense it would be hard to find the difference in me. In another sense, though, God strengthened a desire in me to be instrumental in the development of the people around me."

Corky's impressive list of banking, educational, and civic attainments are too extensive to tell here, yet he dismisses them all with the modest explanation that he's a "people person." He also praises God for revealing the importance of finding His purpose for Corky's immensely active and influential life:

"The neatest part of my business life is when I keep my eyes focused on God. Despite a really busy schedule, there's still time to develop in-depth relationships and experience growth in this way.

"I always did invest in people. Now I'm learning how much others have invested in me. Christian friends had prayed for me as long as fifteen and eighteen years before I accepted Christ!"

The day I discovered my own purpose in life, I recall at first feeling actual dismay about it; I didn't enjoy that widening horizon one bit!

Actually I thought God and I long since had settled that my vocation was Christian writing. How blessed could I get? I truly love my work and praise God for it every day. However, when I sought God's *purpose* for me, He seemed to say I was to become a communicator.

What did that mean? Christian writing, after all, does some pretty important communicating! I asked the Lord to explain. At length I began to realize He wanted me to be willing to communicate by any and all means He might provide—not just writing, but even teaching or speaking if He should choose.

At first I argued silently. This did no good, for God reminded me of several occasions on which I'd turned down invitations to speak with the excuse that I was a terrible speaker and would help them get someone better. If anyone asked me to teach, I'd say I didn't have the gift of teaching.

Then, on January 3, 1976, God not only zapped me, but my husband as well. Friends had invited us to hear Norvel Hayes, a well-known Christian layman, speak at a Full Gospel Businessmen's Fellowship International breakfast. After giving a talk that electrified his fifteen hundred listeners, Brother Hayes issued a series of altar calls—three of them!

First Al and I prayed, with the rest of the congregation, for those who went forward to commit their lives to Christ. Then Norvel asked people to commit their finances to God: "Some of you are cheating the Lord," he said, and many men surged forward to ask God to oversee their financial affairs. Finally he gave the altar call that seemed to touch scores of hearts that day: "Some of you never have given your talents to God. You're holding out on Him. He wants to use you, but you won't offer Him what you have."

"I had the strangest desire to answer that altar call," Al told me later, as he drove us home. "I can't understand why. I committed my life and business and everything else I have to God a long time ago."

"Me too, but I almost couldn't stay in my seat," I confessed. "It was as though the Lord wanted to pull me to the altar. But that doesn't make much sense, because I gave Him full charge over anything I ever write for the rest of my life."

The subject didn't go away. By the time we'd arrived home, Al and I decided to pray until the Lord revealed to our hearts if He wanted to *develop* in us talents we didn't even know we had. I felt certain that wasn't the answer, but we could think of no other avenue to pursue that might still the tug at our hearts.

That afternoon God moved first in Al. It seemed Al felt called to rejoin the Sanctuary Choir, which he'd left a year earlier when our schedule became hectic. "I really don't see why, since I can't read music and they can't possibly need me very much in a choir of a hundred voices," Al said, "but I'll obey."

Three weeks later he was elected choir president.

To my surprise, the moment I queried God about any undeveloped talents in myself, I immediately knew I was not to turn down any more requests for me to speak or teach. "But I'm terrible! I'm totally untrained!" I wailed tearfully.

The very next day someone came to me and told me God had instructed her to ask me to teach, and within a week I'd been asked to speak to three groups—one out of state. I was sufficiently unnerved to enroll in a professional speaking course with a highly trained instructor, a video camera, and a live audience—a challenge I still shudder to remember.

None of this came easily. At first, speaking or teaching gave me cold chills, but the warmth of Christian love soon thawed me out. Still I occasionally rebelled before the Lord. "Why this?" I'd ask Him, until one day I received a beautiful answer.

"You're a communicator," He told me once more. That time the word clicked; *communicator*—is that not akin to the purpose He assigns to His own Son? Jesus, after all, is the perfect Communicator—the One who came to show us the Father. How wonderful to inherit some tiny part of His calling!

The Bible tells us that God's ways are higher than our ways. He wants to help you and me know what those ways are—help us climb to a higher plane that we presently can see.

Today, seek the Lord for your highest purpose. Ask Him to reveal His desires to you, not just in terms of vocation but also your entire life. Ask Him to show you bigger plans than you can envision at this time. And when He does, pray about them and prepare to obey God's leading.

When this is done, you might record it for yourself. On a sheet of paper, write:

My Portrait of Purpose

1. The most important objective I could achieve in my lifetime is:
2. Here's how I believe this lifelong achievement would benefit:
   A. God's Kingdom
   B. My family
   C. Business or community
   D. My friends
   E. My country
3. Am I willing to change my life to achieve this purpose?
4. I will change my life in these ways:

_____

(Signature)   (Date)

You might want to share with someone close to you the disclosures of purpose you just received from God. Did you discover a new truth about yourself? Were there any surprises?

You also might want to think of two or three people in public life or others you know whose lives demonstrate great purpose. Do these people appear to possess special power? Joy? Good health?

It's exciting and almost overwhelming to discover our high calling of God in Christ Jesus. God wants to call each one of us according to His purposes.

That's full-time living!

5

In Living Color

*How to achieve the vibrant life
you envision.*

Identifying my purpose in life is one thing, bringing it about, quite another. How do I get there from here?

"It only took one evening to discover what God wants me to do with my life," one woman observed, "but it would take years of education and hard work to make it happen. What's the use of wishing?"

In her case, wishing proved quite useful. Anne, as we'll call her, described her life and her personality as "mostly wishy-washy shades of gray, with a few splashes of red." When she spoke of interior design, however, which she'd come to realize must be her calling, her somewhat retiring personality changed abruptly.

Anne's self-study revealed that almost every aspect of her life's experience had contributed to her growing interest in design. When she spoke of the challenge and "aliveness" she feels when she works with colors and fabrics and furnishings, her voice became animated and her body tensed with excitement.

"I love it, but I'm just an amateur. Aside from a couple of college art courses, I've had no formal training; and unless I returned to school, I couldn't stand a chance in the profession.

"But don't tell me to go back to school," she warned. "I'm not sure I could handle it. I don't have enough time, money, or self-confidence."

Less than a year later, however, Anne was on her way. She quit wishing and began seeking. Not only did she seek God's will for her life in a new and intensified fashion, but she began seeking out opportunities to advance herself toward her calling—that of creating beautiful environments.

Here's how she did it.

First, Anne prayed. She asked God to show her why she'd "always dabbled in rooms," and she continued to ask until some answers came clear. "It dawned on me that beauty is not only important to me, but to God Himself," she explained. "It's essential to everyone's soul, whether we realize it or not.

"The Lord began to give me wisdom when I asked for it. For example, He reminded me of a room I furnished at a time when I had almost no money; I used orange-crate furniture and coordinated printed sheets for cushions and draperies. I was proud of that room!

"He helped me see again what I already knew—it doesn't require big sums of money to design a happy surrounding, but it does take vision. He showed me I have a knack for seeing possibilities 'in living color.' "

Next, Anne asked God to show her how she could use her gift to further His Kingdom. She asked Him to give her an opportunity to use her talent for His glory, and the answer turned up almost immediately.

"My first design project after that prayer turned out to

be my pastor's office suite, of all places," Anne chuckled. "One day I really looked at those offices and mentally redid them—new paint, freshly covered chairs, smart window treatments.

"Impulsively, I blurted out that I wished they'd turn me loose and let me do my thing in those rooms. Wow! I couldn't believe I'd said it, but you should have seen the dear man's face light up at my offer—especially when I showed him we could do it with only minor bends in the budget."

Not only did Anne enjoy updating her pastor's surroundings, but he termed the transformation "a miracle" and recommended her talents to another businessman who needed his offices decorated. This man, impressed by Anne's sensible approach to the job he assigned her, gladly recommended her to several other potential clients, and he also persuaded her to donate her expertise to a clubhouse his civic group was building to benefit inner-city boys.

As if all this weren't encouragement enough, Anne's biggest thrill was still to come. One of the men involved in building the boys' clubhouse owned the finest furniture store in town. He noticed Anne's volunteer work, was impressed by her sensible ideas and positive attitudes, and offered her a designer's post in his firm.

"That bowled me over," Anne said. "I explained that I didn't possess formal qualifications for the job, but he still hired me. I love the work, of course, and I'm learning new things every day. Besides that, the company pays my tuition for evening-school courses in design. One of these years I'll be a full-fledged professional with all the credentials!"

Was Anne lucky? Did this series of events just fall in place? She emphatically disagreed with that idea. "When I told God what I wanted and asked Him what to do about it, He began to show me some positive ideas to replace my negative doubts," she explained. "He couldn't begin to guide me toward the big desire of my heart, however, until I started really meaning business with Him."

You and I, like Anne, also can learn to "see the possibilities in living color." A good way to do this is to take pencil and paper and begin now to sketch in words the picture of our lives we'd like to see full-blown ten years from today.

This exercise could prove not only exciting for you, but enormously productive as well. However, it's important to do two things: First, *think big*—and second, *be specific*. Take time to spell out every aspect of your plan in exact and elaborate detail. Ask God to illuminate your imagination. The more specifically you plan and think, the more likely you'll be to work your plan to its successful completion.

Let's go. Think big! Be specific!

How I'd Like My Life to Be Ten Years From Today

1. MY SPIRITUAL LIFE TEN YEARS FROM TODAY
   a. What do I want God to do for me?
   b. What do I want to offer God?
   c. What gift or talent would I like God to develop in my life?

2. MY HOME LIFE TEN YEARS FROM TODAY
   a. What things do I want to provide for my family and myself?
   b. What kind of house will we live in?

   c. How will we spend our leisure time and our vacations?

   d. Any special education goals?

   e. Should we plan family reunions? Where?

   f. Family worship time? Who will lead? What will we include?

3. MY WORK LIFE TEN YEARS FROM TODAY

   a. What level of income do I want to attain?

   b. What level of responsibility?

   c. What new job skills?

   d. What professional achievements do I hope to attain?

   e. As a housewife, would I like to phase into the job market part time or full time?

   f. As a businessman, would I like to go into business for myself?

   g. Do I need to start planning to cut back on my workload in preparation for retirement?

4. MY PERSONAL LIFE TEN YEARS FROM TODAY

   a. How old will our children be?

   b. What activities will I be involved in?

   c. Do I want further education? What kind?

   d. New job or profession?

   e. New forms of recreation? Hobbies?

   f. What sort of church responsibility would I enjoy?

   g. Community work?

   h. What worthwhile causes do I want to help?

5. MY MONETARY STATUS TEN YEARS FROM TODAY

   a. Will I own a house or other property?

    b. Do I want to make any large purchases—a boat, vacation home, a trip around the world?

    c. Will I need extra help in my household or my business? New equipment for home or business?

    d. Do I foresee monetary needs for God's work— missions, work abroad, aiding seminary students, or traveling for Christian purposes?

6. LIST ANY OTHER REQUIREMENTS OR DESIRES NOT COV-ERED IN THE FOREGOING CATEGORIES. BE AS SPECIFIC AS POSSIBLE.

Now take a good look at that portrait of ten years hence. Does it excite you? It should! The wonderful thing about those pages of yours is, your blueprint is something God would like to see you achieve.

Doctor William C. Menninger, the world-famous psychiatrist from Topeka, Kansas, believes that each of us should give our life a periodic checkup. He asks:

> Do you know whether you are going in the right direction, and most of all where you want to go?
>
> Not just in your business alone, but in the important personal areas: the atmosphere in your home, your relations with the members of your family, your own feeling of status and worth-wileness in life, your own dignity and your own integrity.

Ouida Canaday, one of Georgia's best-known artists, took just such a life-changing personal checkup some years ago. It netted her a new career, a total change of direction, and three trips around the world!

"I had been a successful commercial artist for eighteen years, working under constant pressure, tension, and deadlines," Ouida told me. "One day I decided I'd had it; I told myself there must be more to life than making pantyhose layouts!

"I decided to go to the mountains for a few days by myself, just to take stock. It was the first time in my life I'd been alone. Since I'd married on my eighteenth birthday, going straight from the arms of my family into the arms of my husband, I'd never had an opportunity to get away by myself and figure out what I wanted and needed in life.

"When you work for yourself, you don't say no, and you don't punch a time clock, so I was working seven days a week, eighteen hours a day. I was so physically exhausted that when I got to my mountain retreat, I slept for three days and three nights."

Ouida took ample time to decide what she wanted her life to include. "My choice was clear-cut—either money or happiness," she explained. "I decided to make a total change in my life and my work. The first thing I did when I returned home was begin to organize my first trip around the world, a trip that included three other women.

"We four gals traveled, without our husbands, with no difficulty and no inharmony whatever. We took almost three months to sketch our way around the world. It helped us realize we aren't as dependent upon our environment or other individuals as we think we are.

"When I returned, I stopped all commercial art and began teaching art classes. I realized there's a tremendous need for the kind of teaching I'm doing. It's more than art;

I want to show women how to bring out their talents, to venture and experiment, to discover themselves.

"I've been able to do this for myself. My own paintings reflect definite progressions from one stage of experience to another, and I like to see these women move along too."

The once-sheltered artist-housewife changed into a woman who didn't hesitate to pack a couple of drip-dry dresses among her dozens of sketchpads and pencils to trek off alone to such places as North Africa, Libya, Malta, Afghanistan, Pakistan, and Siberia, for example.

"From there I entered Bhukara, Samarkand, the Khyber Pass, Mongolia, Outer Mongolia, and the Gobi Desert," Ouida related, "took the Trans-Siberian Railroad and went across and caught a Russian boat to Japan. I met a newspaper reporter—an older lady—and we stayed in Japan three weeks, living like the Japanese: eating raw fish, sleeping on the floor, and having a ball."

Extraordinary? Ouida thinks not. "It's like starting a diet," she said. "You really have to see yourself as you are and as you *could* be. When it becomes more uncomfortable to stay as you are than it would be to change, then you change.

"I learned I could change. I believe every woman needs to get out on her own and figure things out for herself. When you can figure out the rate of monetary exchange in Timbuktu or argue with a native taxi driver, you may feel insecure, you may be nervous, but that's good. When you work out your problems yourself and learn how marvelous people are in the other countries of the world, learn how to communicate in smiles and handclasps instead of words, you learn there are no real barriers between you and the other people of the world.

"There should be no barrier between you and your Self, either!"

Where such a barrier exists, it helps to get alone with God and seek His purpose and direction as we seek our own true, bottom-line desires for life. Again and again, men and women have described to me their adventures with the Lord as they began to visualize something much bolder, bigger, newer, more pleasing and astonishing than they'd ever before been able to imagine for their lives.

That's thinking in full-time living color. Try it for yourself. Ask God to help you think in bold and beautiful terms. Ask for His wisdom.

He wants to help you trade in your black-and-white existence for vivid, full-color life—radiant as a rainbow!

6

Winning With Goals

Goals can change your life.

Goals can change your life.

Do you believe that? Here's an easy way you can test that statement right now: Simply state *out loud* your own most immediate or important goal. Take one minute to decide what it might be.

Now, did you pass the test?

Could you think of any goal at all? If so, you rank with a tiny minority indeed, according to Napoleon Hill, author of *Think and Grow Rich.* Mr. Hill recorded an amazing statistic when he wrote that 98 percent of the entire population fails to set goals.

What are goals, anyhow? And how can goals change my life?

Please notice three things goals are:

1. *Goals are specific.* Goals include definite, specific actions we intend to take.

2. *Goals are measurable.* Goals allow us to measure our progress. They may be quantitative (how much we intend

73

to do and how often) or stated in terms of time (how soon we intend to accomplish them).

3. *Goals relate to a definite period.* Goals are specific time targets—an intent to achieve a particular result during that period. Your *objectives* may be pursued for indefinite times in the future; your *goals* are what you determine to do within a specific planning period to move you toward your objective.

How can goals change our lives?

Goals tap into the power within us and actually seem to call forth far more energy than we dream we possess. Goals act as spark plugs to get us going. Goals propel us toward full-time living!

Please notice, *purpose* is long-range—your big, overall picture. *Goals* represent your short-range future—the living you'll do this month, this week, and today. Therefore, through learning how to set goals, *I can dramatically alter what happens to me next!*

Let's see how this can work for you. Start with a calendar, a pen, and several sheets of paper. At the top of your paper write:

MY GOALS FOR (MONTH)

1. Jot down the most important things you must do this month.

2. List things you want to do this month.

3. Place dates by items with deadlines; for example, beside "pay bills" write "fifteenth" or whatever is appropriate.

4. Assign deadline dates for remaining items.

5. Divide items into Week One, Week Two, Week Three and Week Four.

Before you decide this exercise is too simplistic, take a critical look at what you just wrote. Do you like what you see? Examine your goals for balance. Is all the heavy business at one end of the calendar and much of the blank space at the other end?

If so, let's examine that upcoming month for its creative possibilities, keeping in mind the fact that your Self is a trinity—mind, body, and spirit. Ideally, each part of that Self gets "fed" each day; in reality, however, most of us ignore at least one element in that important trio.

Now try this: Survey your month, week by week, to see if your plans will serve *your whole Self.* Take Week One. What do you plan to feed your *mind* that week? A good chunk of research, perhaps? Will you set up your club's programs for the coming year? Balance the family budget? Give a talk? Read a stimulating book? *Your mind needs daily exercise.*

Second, think about your *body.* Do you exercise your body each day? Take the family for a walk after dinner? Will you mow the lawn on Saturday, or take a swim? Will you use that body this week, really stretch it, limber it, tone it, put it through its paces? It sounds quite obvious, but *we should use and appreciate our physical bodies every day of the year.*

Also, plan to be good to your *spirit!* Because you have the mind of Christ, feed on His Word. Did you schedule time for regular prayer and praise, time for leisurely "aloneness" with your Father? Will you dawdle along an autumn-dappled trail for an hour some afternoon? Take your son for a walk in the rain? Sip lemonade on the terrace and admire the stars? Hear a concert? Teach your grandchild to sing "Silent Night"? *Be sure to feed your spirit!*

My spirit will live forever. Naturally it longs to be linked, day by day and hour by hour, to the One who is the same yesterday, today, and forever.

Remember how you felt as a child, when a birthday-party invitation arrived in the mail? It gave you something to look forward to. Your goals should do exactly the same thing!

Goals provide a healthy expectation of finding something good just around the corner. As we list on paper those ideas we want to bring to reality, as well as those things we know we *must* accomplish, we begin to tingle with the knowledge that things are about to happen.

God wants to help us with that goal setting, and surely He will help bring our plans to fruition. The Bible tells us: "A man's mind plans his way, but the Lord directs his steps and makes them sure" (Proverbs 16:9 AMPLIFIED).

Doctor Maxwell Maltz, author of *Psycho-Cybernetics,* writes that human beings are engineered as goal-seeking mechanisms. "We are built that way," he explains. "When we have no personal goals which we are interested in and mean something to us, we have to go around in circles, feel lost, and find life itself aimless and purposeless. We are built to conquer environment, solve problems, achieve goals—and we find no real satisfaction or happiness in life without obstacles to conquer and goals to achieve.

"People who say that life is not worthwhile are really saying that they have no personal goals which are worthwhile. Get yourself a goal worth working for," he wrote. "Better still, get yourself a project. Decide what you want out of a situation. Always have something ahead to look forward to."

Ask yourself, what am I looking forward to? Have I spelled out my goals sufficiently clearly? Do I, in fact, at this moment, anticipate something good that's going to happen to me—something specific—by a certain specified date?

The Bible gives us a wonderful method for making good things happen: "Commit thy works unto the Lord, and thy thoughts shall be established." (Proverbs 16:3 KJV). I'd like to share with you how this works for me.

First, I always work from a calendar—a five-year calendar. Years ago my father taught me the wisdom of trying to project mentally the possible effects of today's efforts or decisions. "Think ahead," he advised. "How will this affect your life five years from now?" At that time I was a high-school student. Daddy helped me see I must measure my decisions about school courses, after-school job, piano practice, and helping Mother with housework against how these experiences would help me five years later, as a college girl.

That started a habit that still works for me. It's fun to take certain goals—writing this book, for example—and estimate how they might build toward what God and I envision my life to be five years hence.

This thought pattern can head off potential mistakes, too. A young woman, still in her twenties, gained three pounds. "I projected five years ahead and saw myself fifteen pounds heavier. Ten years from now, gaining at that rate, I'd weigh thirty pounds more than I want," she told me.

"It was easy to decide to cut out colas and candy and begin jogging every morning. My goal is to keep my body at its normal weight all my life."

I like to break the current year of my five-year calendar into seasons: winter, spring, summer, and fall. It's wonderful to sketch in the calendar highlights of each. Try it. It's fun. For example:

Winter: New wallpaper for my office. Shop for spring clothes. Complete this book before time to spade garden or set out pansy plants.

Spring: Renew passport. Schedule speaking dates. Special Holy Week worship. Garden, garden, garden!

Summer: Think about fall book. Visit our special island. Clean house thoroughly. Organize storage space. Visit our parents.

Fall: September, plan family Christmas. Israel trip in November, home by Thanksgiving. Work on book. New Year's Eve praise party?

There you have it, in rough. With the stellar events of each season delineated, it remains only to assign each five-star item to its day of the week on the calendar—or at least, try to estimate. Then I begin to fill in around those superstars, setting out special goals as methodically as I'd set out larkspur and daisies and chrysanthemums—by the season.

The plan works; it works because it becomes almost as predictable as the seasons—with big, comforting time gaps to accommodate the unpredictables that surely will come.

The plan works because of satisfying built-in personal goals that literally push it forward. Those goals will bring a predictably high ratio of good results per week, month, and year. Good goals, because they help balance my life, will continue to increase the quality of life for me, my family, and others I love.

Above all else, setting goals correctly makes it possible for me, like Jesus, to "minister rather than be ministered unto"—and that's full-time living!

It's great to know how to schedule my goals, but let's admit it's often hard to *determine* those goals in the first place. How in the world do I figure out *what* I hope to do this month, much less *when* I'll do it?

Here are some ways you can determine your goals. These methods, incidentally, help you coordinate today's efforts with your big purpose—something we should keep in mind constantly.

First, *find out what you really want above all else.* After you determine your goal, you can visualize it in "living color." Picture what you want to do and how you'll do it. Let your Father help with this. Go ahead and get excited, too—it won't hurt!

Then, *do your homework.* Do some research on yourself, your idea, the possibilities and pitfalls. Get information from the public library, expertise from friends, brochures from your travel agent. Get your facts together, then analyze them. Put them in workable order, then determine how you're going to accomplish your goal.

Next, *set a time schedule.* Become a bit inflexible here. Deadlines help keep you on the path. Figure out exactly how you're going to work your plan, and time each step of it. Decide to start now. Believe in what you're doing, and believe in yourself. Tell yourself, "I can do all things through Christ which strengtheneth me" (Philippians 4:13).

Little goals are soon accomplished and bring confidence-boosting feelings of success. Medium-sized goals give you solid evidence of "getting somewhere." Big goals make you stretch yourself in mind, body, and spirit. They can produce fantastic dividends in terms of knowing God. After all, we must collaborate with Him if we're to achieve anything really great!

To inject some instant anticipation in your life, decide on a good goal today. Don't hesitate, just do it. Sometimes our "Time of Your Life" classes bog down right here; everyone gets stumped by the simple question, what is your next goal?

One lady, married to an insurance agent, said her goal was for him to meet his sales quota and qualify them to take a trip to Hawaii. Everyone laughed, but maybe that's a legitimate goal for her. We might assume that her interest in his progress, her pep talks, her shopping ahead of time for muumuus, just might make *him* try harder for *her*.

As you think about your goals, remember to set time limits. One man decided to try jogging every day for a month or until he had cardiac arrest, whichever came first.

After two weeks, our hero changed goals; he simply wanted to run a mile without pausing at intervals to limp and gasp for breath. After three weeks of daily sacrifice, he had achieved that goal—ever so proudly!—and added a new one. He wanted to persuade his wife to join him on the jogging track before the month was out.

By deciding at the outset that he'd give jogging a thirty-day trial, our friend built in his eventual success. By the end of two weeks he saw he *could* jog, despite his initial reluctance; by the end of the third, he was jogging steadily; and before his thirty days elapsed, he convinced his wife of the benefits he was receiving and converted her to the idea as well.

Remember, it's the goal itself that turns us on, and not necessarily the size of it. Any goal at all—even an apparently insignificant one—provides stimulus and challenge.

A cute girl named Jeannie confessed she felt as though her life were in something of a slump. When she worked out her Present Life Profile, she saw she had very little "payoff" prepared, considering how hard she works. She decided to set some new goals.

"Actually, one was an old goal—that of becoming an airline stewardess. A couple of years ago I applied to several companies, but at that time nobody was hiring. I let myself get discouraged and forgot the idea.

"Last week I dusted off that old goal and reapplied to every airline I could find. This time I plan to be persistent. Just deciding that, going through the effort of having new photos made, filling out job-application forms, and trudging all over town with them, got me really excited about life. It usually takes a while to get a job with an airline, however, so I gave myself another goal to work on in the meantime. This second goal already has paid off!"

Jeannie wanted to sing. In fact, she longed to join a dynamic group sponsored by her church—a large choir of young men and women whose singing customarily won them standing ovations, but whose personal ministries seemed equally blessed.

"It took every bit of nerve I had to ask to join that group," she told me. "A lot of those people do concert dates and recordings, and I can't even read music! They told me to come on, and the next night I joined a sight-reading class.

"The week after I joined this fantastic bunch of people, we had a weekend retreat in the mountains, with singing and skiing and worship services and getting to know one another. I found some neat new friends, learned to ski some, and started a diet. I'm having the time of my life!"

Goals can change your life. Goals are essential to winning, and God wants to help you establish some winning goals.

After all, He did not create a race of losers. As one Christian put it, "God don't sponsor no flops." With God's help, you can begin winning with goals today!

7

Playing to Your Strengths

Making the most of what you are.

Do you know the secret of playing to your strengths? Do you know how to concentrate on the tremendous force within you and ignore your lesser strengths? Have you learned to focus on what you *are* instead of what you're *not?*

The man who knows God and realizes the power of God in his life can accomplish his goals. He knows how to follow the biblical injunction to:

> Roll your works upon the Lord—commit and trust them wholly to Him; [He will cause your thoughts to become agreeable to His will, and] so shall your plans be established and succeed.
>
> Proverbs 16:3 AMPLIFIED

You and I can do that. We can roll our works upon the Lord and begin fulfilling His big plans for our lives. There's no question that God intends us to meet our goals to a glorious degree.

There's a question about *me*, however; the question is, am I totally committed to my goal, or am I saying one thing and living another? The Bible says:

> If any of you lack wisdom, let him ask of God, that giveth to all men liberally, and upbraideth not; and it shall be given him. But let him ask in faith, nothing wavering. For he that wavereth is like a wave of the sea driven with the wind and tossed. For let not that man think that he shall receive any thing of the Lord. A double minded man is unstable in all his ways.
>
> James 1:5–8 KJV

Am I double-minded? As any doctor can attest, hospitals and medical waiting rooms are jammed with people whose physical ailments stem from division within themselves. Disorganization and lack of goals can produce psycho-somatic illness—*stress diseases*, the experts call them—because when body, mind, and spirit fail to function in harmony, illness results.

We've all seen it. Each of us can cite examples of lives that produce illness due to disorganization and lack of goals:

- The alcoholic housewife who has no goal other than to drink.
- The overweight executive with doctor's orders to stop smoking, who says he has no time for exercise.

- The teenager who dates several nights a week and watches late television the other evenings, then comes down with mononucleosis.
- The married woman with a career, who shops on Saturdays and cleans house on Sundays. She has no time for church or normal fellowship.
- The retired person who naps a lot, has no scheduled activities, no paying job, and wonders why he doesn't sleep well at night.

The good news, however, is that God can help the world's most confirmed loser—can teach him how to win—by teaching him to play to his strengths. The truth is, you and I, through the power of God, can overcome any circumstance in our lives. We can learn to do this.

It's important to seek God's wisdom and to ask for the mind of Christ. Then we can see ourselves truthfully. We can quit kidding ourselves, making excuses, and allowing ourselves to be double-minded. When we can begin to explore some possible reasons for our lifelong failure to attain some of our reasonable goals, we can learn to face our faults realistically and without self-hatred.

God wants to help with this. His Holy Bible is crammed with promises toward the man or woman who would learn to be godly. The Bible is alive with exciting, eternal goals; indeed, it contains every principle for personal success ever given to man.

Read the Bible. Ask God to show you those Scriptures you need, then watch what happens!

While the Bible reveals those personal qualities which lead us to success, it's equally faithful to point out the opposite: those traits which doom man to failure, illness, sin, and unrequited plans. God warns us about:

- Vanity
- Failure to be teachable
- Selfishness
- Anger and hot temper
- Laziness
- Greed
- Unwillingness to serve
- Pride
- Envy and jealousy
- Intemperance
- Refusal to work "as unto the Lord"

Each of these failure traits, which God terms *sin,* or *missing the mark,* can result from a lack of goals. Holy goals, established in our hearts by God Himself, faithfully prayed over, joyfully desired and received, will lead us into new and wonderfully disciplined lives.

One way we can begin playing to our strengths is to take a good, hard look at any weaknesses of character God would like to help us overcome.

What character traits hinder me from reaching my goals? What bit of double-mindedness does the Lord want to root out of me? Actually, am I my own worst enemy?

If so, it's time to make another contract with myself. I will decide to turn loose of my lifelong "right" to fail, and I will put that decision in writing! At the top of a sheet of paper, write:

What I Need to Do Right Now

TO STEER MYSELF TOWARD SUCCESS

(List some things which could add power to your life right now. Name specific activities.)

TO AVOID FAILURE

(Name some things you're now doing that work against your chances for success: for example, habitual oversleeping, failure to plan, procrastination, and so on.)

TODAY I HAVE DECIDED TO:

(Here list the steps you have decided to take.)

_____
(Name)   (Date)

Full-time living features consistent achievements. These result from the goals you choose, and, to achieve any goal, you must commit yourself to making your best efforts. It's important to make an all-out, conscious and unconscious commitment. Mind, body, and spirit should work together harmoniously. I must be unified within myself and with my God.

Full-time living also implies *balanced* living.

Ask yourself: Is my present life well balanced? If not, what does it lack? Could you, with intelligent goal setting, kick something else out of the present schedule to put that "new thing" in?

Perhaps you remember the little Sunday-school acronym:

J–esus first
O–thers second
Y–ourself also

That's a simple, effective formula for a balanced life, and it produces the JOY it promises! As we set goals to harness these lives of ours, as we attempt to grow into new discipline and serenity, it's important to aim for a better balance in our activities and, consequently, our personalities.

As you know, the unbalanced life inevitably becomes the unsuccessful life. Show me a woman who lives for her children, and I'll show you a person whose spirit is dying.

Show me a man who is married to his work, and I believe his family life must be stunted.

Show me a child whose purpose is that of acting as family-entertainment center, who is dressed and fussed over and catered to, with no expectation of his giving anything in return, and I'll show you a child with very little sense of self-worth.

I must learn to balance my life; it will no more balance itself than will my marvelous Swiss watch be able to correct its own timing mechanism. But who will teach me to correct my own timing? Obviously I must turn myself over to Jesus—the way, the truth and the life.

Jesus, others, and yourself make full-time living not only possible, but beautifully practicable. Sometimes, however, that third member of the group—yourself—gets his name left out of the pot. Often it's the superconscientious Christian, devoted to Jesus and to others, who wonders why life is going flat. Where is the joy? Why is he tired all the time? What's wrong with him?

It's time to balance that life! Jesus told us to "love thy neighbor as thyself." He knew we couldn't continually pour from an empty pitcher; He knew our Father meant love to be received, as well as given. After all, if I can't receive love, how can I give it? And if I cannot love myself, how can I love you?

One way to make sure you're loving yourself is to check and see what you've done for yourself lately. Should you give yourself a gift? Would you give yourself a gift or do yourself a kindness if you were someone else you know?

Often the flatness and stress in my life can be traced to a certain insensitivity on my part to my own needs. God expects me to correct that sin now.

But you say, I can't. I know my present life-style is weakening and self-defeating, but there's nothing I can do about it right now. There's not enough time. There's not enough money. There's not enough of me to go around.

If I stop smoking, I'll gain weight. If I took a vacation with the family, I might miss out on some business opportunities. If I don't take care of my daughter's clothes, she'll look like a slob.

It takes some of us a long time to accept the answer to that sort of dilemma. First, take it to the Lord. Jesus said, "Take my yoke upon you, and learn of me . . . . For my yoke is easy, and my burden is light" (Matthew 11:29, 30 KJV).

Second, God expects me to take it to my husband. Why? Because the Bible says he is to love me ". . . as Christ also loved the church . . . ." (Ephesians 5:25 KJV.) Many of us self-sufficient wives forget that God expects us to allow our husbands to love and help us when we're tired, dejected, and feeling defeated. Just as Jesus gave His church all He had, God expects my husband to minister to me with that same all-out, tender concern.

Betty Foy Sanders, formerly the first lady of Georgia, remembers a time a dozen years ago when her husband did just that. Governor and Mrs. Carl E. Sanders ranked among America's youngest and most admired couples in high office. Both were well prepared for their respective roles, enjoyed public life, and served with distinction.

Despite her well-publicized talents and youthful energy, however, Betty's role as first lady—a full-time occupation apart from her duties as wife and mother of two preteen youngsters—eventually began to rob her of something important. "There's no time for me at all. I love being first lady, but I feel I'm in danger of losing touch with myself. I need something other than responsibility, something to relax me," she told her husband.

The governor advised his wife to play to her strengths; specifically, he suggested that she take art lessons, since Betty had majored in fine arts at the university.

"I thought it was a terrible suggestion!" she said. "Art takes time, and I couldn't count on even an hour a day to myself. It also takes space, and I couldn't find any real space at all, believe it or not, in that big, old, official mansion."

She did it anyhow. Despite motherhood, wifehood and countless official duties, Betty somehow squeezed art lessons into her schedule and disciplined herself to work every day she possibly could. Long before her husband left office she held a showing of her paintings, which won excellent reviews.

She continues to study, paint, travel, and exhibit her work. It gives her satisfaction to realize that her own active participation in the arts at the time her husband was governor placed a spotlight on all Georgia's arts. "I worked hard to boost the status of art in Georgia, and we got some things done," she says. Actually, her list of accomplishments in this area is too long to mention here.

Obviously, she's glad she set that "impossible" goal and glad she persevered. Many people have benefited from that decision, including the Sanders family. "Carl often says he admires the fact that I can go to the studio and get away from it all, then return to the family totally refreshed," she says.

Balancing my life makes great sense. Not only does it increase my own peace of mind, effectiveness, and joy, but it also enhances my family's welfare. The apostle Paul said, "if one member of the body suffers, all suffer." Conversely, when one member strengthens, all strengthen.

I *can* achieve my goals. Here are some excellent ways in which I can begin to play to my strengths:

1. I will review my goals prayerfully at regular, decided-upon intervals. (I do this at the beginning of each new month.)

2. I'll honor them with my serious attention. If my goal is success and I'm dawdling my way to failure, who am I kidding?

3. I must visualize myself achieving my goal.

4. I'll list on paper the specific steps I need to take. I'll give myself deadlines.

5. Today I'll write that letter or place the phone call that will help me take the next step toward my goal.

6. I'll plan to have recreation and fun every week. I'll attempt to balance my life-style.

7. My goals should represent something I really want to do, not just something I think I ought to do. I am responsible to God for my own life. I will consult Him and my own heart before consulting others.

8. Most important, I will remember the words of Jesus Christ:

> And I say unto you, Ask, and it shall be given you; seek, and ye shall find; knock, and it shall be opened unto you. For every one that asketh receiveth; and he that seeketh findeth; and to him that knocketh it shall be opened. If a son shall ask bread of any of you that is a father, will he give him a stone? or if he ask a fish, will he for a fish give him a serpent? Or if he shall ask an egg, will he offer him a scorpion? If ye then, being evil, know how to give good gifts unto your children: how much more shall your heavenly Father give the Holy Spirit to them that ask him?
>
>   Luke 11:9–13 KJV

Jesus points the way toward full-time living. Jesus came to show me the Father. And because He did, I can confidently expect my goals, which come from Him, to bear much fruit. Jesus said:

> Abide in me, and I in you. As the branch cannot bear fruit of itself, except it abide in the vine; no more can ye, except ye abide in me. I am the vine, ye are the branches: He that abideth in me, and I in him, the same bringeth forth much fruit: for without me ye can do nothing. If a man abide not in me, he is cast forth as a branch, and is withered; and men gather them, and cast them into the fire, and they are burned. If ye abide in

me, and my words abide in you, ye shall ask what
ye will, and it shall be done unto you. Herein is
my Father glorified, that ye bear much fruit; so
shall ye be my disciples.

John 15:4–8 KJV

Lord, be our true strength. Help us bear good fruit!

8

First Things First

Letting God control your time.

When I popped in on Dick Schneider one spring morning four years ago, I apologized right away for interrupting his work. I seldom get to New York City, his office at Guideposts Magazine was conveniently close, so I hoped . . . .

"You're not an interruption. God doesn't send interruptions; He sends opportunities," my friend chid me, smiling. His serene attitude in the face of a heaped-up desk really bothered me; I didn't quite buy what he was saying.

"Magazine editors don't have time for pop calls," I began again, somewhat crossly, but Dick shook his head.

"The Lord controls my time," he said, firmly, and now I believed him. A surge of pure envy shot through me. I felt sure Dick was about to tell me some important truth I really didn't want to hear, and that's exactly what happened.

"The Lord created time," Dick continued, in response to my skeptical look. "He manages time, and I feel He even bends time—when we're in His will."

"What do you mean by that, Dick?"

"As long as we stay in His will, He takes care of everything. When we jump out of His will and try to do things ourselves, that's when we get panicky."

By now the shoe was very close to fitting me, so I attempted to sidestep by asking questions. "You mean you never worry about time? You don't get snowed under? You never miss a deadline?"

Dick swung his chair away from the piled-up desk and gazed out at his slice of Manhattan. "We're all afflicted with the Puritan work ethic that says if we're not doing something every moment, we're to feel guilty," he observed.

"That's not true. Sometimes we need, as our first priority, to be still and know He is God. And sometimes we just need to savor what Lloyd Ogilvie calls 'those moments of Christian serendipity.' "

What Dick said that morning felt okay—for him, I decided. For me, it didn't fit. I figured I'd never reach the state to which he'd arrived, and that part of the conversation annoyed me a little. I decided Dick Schneider managed to stay serene because he had, first, a sweet spirit, and second, someone to answer the telephone. At that point in my life I saw very little likelihood of my acquiring either resource.

Three years later I recalled that episode because a Scripture reached out and grabbed me. I'd read it many times before, of course, but that day it came alive in my understanding and caused me to recall the things Dick told me: "The Lord created time. He manages time, and He'll even bend time—when we're in His will."

The Scripture, Matthew 6:31–34 (KJV), apparently had

nothing to do with that subject. It was that part of Jesus' instructions to His disciples in which He said,

> Therefore take no thought, saying, What shall we eat? or, What shall we drink? or, Wherewithal shall we be clothed? (For after all these things do the Gentiles seek:) for your heavenly Father knoweth that ye have need of all these things. But seek ye first the kingdom of God, and his righteousness; and all these things shall be added unto you. Take therefore no thought for the morrow: for the morrow shall take thought for the things of itself. Sufficient unto the day is the evil thereof.

Since "taking thought" about what I'd eat, drink, or wear was not my problem, I'd never thought before that it might be just as sinful to worry about life's intangibles.

True, I don't hoard food or bother much about clothing (in fact, I hate to shop for clothes). What I did hoard, however, was any small scrap of time or energy. I prided myself on not wasting time. I'd cheerfully give you my last dime if you needed it; on the other hand, I'd hesitate to give you fifteen minutes.

What a horrid self-discovery! How awful to realize I was fully as miserly as any pagan could be when it came to putting my schedule first.

Could it be that God wanted me to trust Him to work out my time problems, as He had for Dick? Would God really bend time for me, as Dick said He would, when I was in His will? More important, was I willing to get into His will about this? I was beginning to see how much I actually idolized my schedule.

Even so, believe it or not, it took a while for me to "seek first the kingdom of God and his righteousness." When I did, of course, "all these things" could be added.

For me or for you, it often boils down to what our mothers taught us about putting first things first. The trouble is, many of us didn't know that meant putting *God's* first things first.

I began to change many of my priorities. Early in this book, you'll recall, I challenged you to discover ways by which you could increase your output—or your leisure and personal time—by 100 percent. Incredibly, allowing God to teach me how to establish my priorities did exactly that for me.

Putting God's first things first eventually teaches us to do only those things we really want to do. That idea floored me, initially. Perhaps you remember Augustine's dictum: "Love God, and do as you please." Jesus said it differently: "The kingdom of God is within you."

For years, such freedom, the freedom of Christ, was something I could neither understand nor accept. It totally contradicted my own, unexamined belief that I exist, in part, to meet other people's expectations and to fill other people's needs.

No wonder it was impossible to imagine a life in which one could mostly do exactly what he feels called to do. Wouldn't that be unthinkably selfish? Instead, life had settled into an endless routine of "meet the need, whatever it might be." Legitimate needs are at every hand; they march in by platoons.

No wonder there's no time left, once I've tried to accommodate myself to the needs and expectations of everyone else I meet, to wonder about God's call on my life.

No wonder there's so little energy left and such pitifully shallow pools of true compassion, sometimes.

Jesus, however, set us quite a different example. He emphasized His intention of serving God, and He ministered with divine, miraculous power. Clearly, however, Jesus was a God pleaser rather than a man pleaser. He sometimes dodged the crowds. After ministering to and feeding the thousands, the Bible says He stepped into a boat and headed away from them; surely they weren't ready for Him to go.

Had Jesus thought as I did, He would have felt guilty about leaving as long as any needed His teaching or His healing touch. But Jesus stayed within the will of the Father. He obeyed His Father implicitly.

At the height of Jesus' ministry, he often withdrew to the desert or the mountains or to a boat on the Sea of Galilee, to be alone with God. Often He had to elude the multitudes in order to do this.

The Bible tells us that Jesus ministered to many thousands of people, but we're not told that He worked without respite as long as any needed teaching, touching, or healing, though obviously all needed His touch.

No, Jesus set the supreme example of how to love God and do as you please. That's why He had time to dine with Mary, Martha, and Lazarus; smile at children; serve fish to His disciples; and turn water into wine at the wedding feast. God gave Jesus, as He gave you and me, plenty of time to be human. He didn't value His Son just for His works!

If only I could get hold of that fully. If only I really did care as much about pleasing my Father as I care about what you think of me. Then I could always put first things first!

While we learn who we are becoming, however, it pays to realize how often our priorities really will be in error. We can only continue to *try* to line up our decisions according to the will of the Father. It takes much practice. As the Bible says, "The fear of the Lord is the beginning of knowledge . . ." (Proverbs 1:7 KJV).

A good way to establish priorities for each day is to arise early and take that day before God in prayer. As the Scripture says, "Early will I seek thee."

During my quiet time I seek the Lord each morning with pen and note pad in hand. I make plans prayerfully, seeking the Bible for additional wisdom. By the end of my prayer time, I've also made a list of the day's assignments for me.

Sometimes I'm astonished at the length of the list, especially when the Lord places on my heart a person or persons to telephone, or some other little, time-consuming errand I could leave off. Often these days, the list contains notations I know I wouldn't have thought of, but I do them without question. It's interesting.

I number the items on my list in what seems to me to be the order of their importance, and then I do them in that order. That's simple enough—and extremely effective— yet so many people never make lists. If you don't plan your day on paper, I'd like to challenge you to try it for one week. I believe a fair trial will convert you!

Often I begin a day with a list two-days long. How will it

all get done? I wonder, but no longer do I rush and hassle and fling unhappy sentences toward my husband about the difficulties of trying to do three things at once.

No, I can't blame my husband. If the yard-long list of things doesn't get done, maybe I missed the Lord. Maybe He didn't tell me to do all that work anyhow. I've noticed that He never directs me to work myself to exhaustion, as I would order myself to do. His priorities seem a lot kinder than mine!

Today, try cooperating with the Lord in setting your priorities. Take each thing you must do as a separate entity and approach it calmly. Imagine the way Jesus would do it; no rushing about, no strained voice on the telephone, no sloppy work or excuses, no procrastination or forgetting.

Because you're willing to give up stress, because you refuse to allow it to build up, you finish each task quickly. You discover, to your surprise, that you've done much more than you imagined you could, and you did it with a minimum expenditure of energy.

That's where the extra time comes from. That's why you can increase your leisure or your output by perhaps 100 percent!

God's priorities for me? I'm finding them throughout the Bible. He doesn't stress time, but He says a lot about love. He doesn't tell me how to schedule, but He says plenty about how to find wisdom. Apparently God isn't as interested in creating efficiency experts for His Kingdom as He is in transforming hearts and lives!

There's a beautiful passage of Scripture that provides me with the dynamics of setting priorities perfectly. I recommend it!

Trust in the Lord with all thine heart; and lean not unto thine own understanding. In all thy ways acknowledge him, and he shall direct thy paths. Be not wise in thine own eyes: fear the Lord, and depart from evil. It shall be health to thy navel, and marrow to thy bones. Honour the Lord with thy substance, and with the firstfruits of all thine increase: So shall thy barns be filled with plenty, and thy presses shall burst out with new wine.

Proverbs 3:5–10 KJV

Acknowledge Him, and He will set your first things first.

9

Your Magic Fifteen Minutes

*Fifteen minutes can open the door
to any goal.*

If you devote just fifteen minutes a day to your dream, it can come true!

That's one of the most powerfully creative facts anyone ever taught me, and it's astoundingly true. You can do almost anything you want to do, if you spend just fifteen minutes a day at it.

I'll give you some examples to back up that claim, but first, let's think about you for a moment. What's the biggest dream of your life? How important is it to you? How much would you give to make it happen?

Would you be willing to give fifteen minutes a day?

Now consider this: In three years you can become expert on any subject you care to study—Chinese art, computer programming, cooking, duck hunting—if you work at it fifteen minutes a day.

In just one year or less you can accomplish some tremendous tasks by investing just fifteen minutes a day. For example, you could:

- Read the entire Bible
- Plant and keep up a small garden
- Become physically fit
- Maintain an active personal correspondence
- Paint a house
- Run one or two miles
- Write a book

You get the picture!

Remembering the day I discovered the magic of fifteen minutes still makes me smile. We'd driven to a small town in the country that hot summer Saturday, to call on a friend who was the town's only doctor.

George not only was a doctor, but an ardent do-it-yourselfer as well. He'd recently bought a sprawling Victorian house and we discovered him sitting in the middle of a room, surrounded by paint cans and a clutter of tools, gazing toward the ceiling and muttering, "That thing's gotta come down!"

We thought he'd flipped—especially when we learned that George intended to repair, repaint, or refurbish every room in that three-story monstrosity by himself.

How long would it take? Where would he find the time? A doctor's life ordinarily doesn't lend itself to large outside projects, so we wondered: How unrealistic could he get?

A quick tour of the already-completed rooms, however, aroused our interest and excitement. I admired a charming "new" bathroom in which George had lowered the ceiling, installed and painted new storage cabinets, hung wallpaper, changed light fixtures, and even provided heated towel bars.

How? "I work fifteen minutes at a time, but never stop

before my time is up," George explained. "That's the secret: Work fifteen minutes a day, without fail."

Later, as we sipped tall glasses of iced tea, George shared the factors that led him to his "magic fifteen minutes" decision. "Since there's no other doctor to help me, I really don't have office hours. Every highway accident, every overturned tractor, every dog-bite or busted arm in a radius of fifty miles demands my services.

"I love this life, but it's murder. With no time off whatever, I found my blood pressure getting out of bounds. I knew I had to make some time for myself.

"One day I decided to take fifteen minutes at a time, whenever I could get them, and I would work on my project, regardless of the telephone. Even if an emergency happened, I'd let it wait—unless it literally was life and death. That was a hard decision to make, but my own life and health depend on my breaking up these long hours I work and siphoning off some of the tension.

"As it turns out, I seldom leave my project. Just knowing I have that fifteen minutes pinned down gives me something to look forward to. I feel I have some control over my life," he explained.

"Using fifteen minutes at a time, *minimum,* you'll be surprised how much time you can squeeze out, some days. If the phone doesn't ring, I might work for forty minutes or two hours. If it does ring, I still get fifteen minutes. I can't lose!"

Still, I was skeptical. I couldn't believe such a simple plan could possibly help me. However, after admiring the evidence—two delightful bathrooms, so far, and a handsomely remodeled kitchen already at the halfway point—I decided to give it a try.

That was more than twenty years ago, and since then I've had great fun with those magic chunks of time. My first project was to tackle a badly neglected flower garden which was choked with weeds. Every time I looked out the dining-room window, I fretted, because I thought I had no time whatever to try to redeem that impossible garden.

That's when I learned how many weeds I could pull in fifteen minutes! It took just one week, snatching a quarter hour here, another there, to get that flower border tidy, neatly mulched, and ready for new transplants.

The beauty of fifteen minutes a day is that it helps me to stop postponing those things I really want or need to do and get them behind me. It banishes discouragement and halts procrastination. The method works on any job or goal that matters to me, whether it's writing this book or cleaning all the kitchen cupboards.

Fifteen minutes a day, I tell myself firmly. If unexpected guests appear and I droop at the thought of losing a writing day, I'm entitled to fifteen minutes—which should result in one page. That's better than nothing, isn't it? Sure it is. One page pushes the job ahead, maintains one's continuity, presents tangible evidence that I mean business with myself. Besides, even one page a day adds up to a book in a very few weeks!

Many grim little jobs really don't deserve more than fifteen minutes a day, anyhow. Done *in toto*, they'd be too much of a bad thing. You know the jobs I mean: filing papers, cleaning closets, polishing silver, tidying a garage or toolshed.

That sort of task, however, makes an enjoyable break from other duties. After a long committee meeting, it might be soothing to polish the coffee service. Tidying a drawer or cupboard seems easy and satisfying after writing a news release. Keeping a list of short-term tasks handy is a good way to vary one's workday and keep the house or office running well.

Large goals—some pleasant, others less so—can be accomplished fifteen minutes at a time. I know a man who prepares his income-tax returns that way. Since he hates the job, he begins early in January and works a few minutes each day until all is shipshape. "I used to do it all in one terrible day just before the deadline," he moaned. "I'd upset the whole house for a week! Now, even stringing it out this way, it never takes as long as I think it will. I get the whole ordeal over during January."

My friend Carole worked out her life's ambition—a trip to England—as a one-year goal, shortly after she'd been flattened by divorce. "When a friend tried to help by suggesting that I take a trip, it made me bitter," Carole said. "I couldn't even afford a trip around the block. Not only did I not have any money, but I didn't have any heart for it."

The friend persisted, however, and challenged Carole to set a goal for herself: She'd work just a few minutes each day in order to visit England one year from then. "It was a wild idea, a crazy thought, but it grabbed me," Carole said. "The first time I walked into a travel agency and emerged with a fistful of folders, I knew I was hooked."

Carole did her homework. Each day she spent part of her lunch hour studying travel plans, accommodations, sight-seeing tours. She checked out books about England from the library and filled a notebook with places and things she *must* see.

Once she'd decided where she wanted to go, how long

she'd stay, and what the trip might cost, Carole and her advisor worked out a strategy. "I had to concentrate on three things: reading about England, buying a few clothes, and accumulating money—quite a bit of money," she said.

Money was the big challenge. With eleven months to work on her goal, Carole estimated just how much she'd have to tuck away each month to make her trip happen. The sum she needed seemed impossible to attain, so she considered postponing the trip—momentarily.

"Do you know what I made myself do to earn my way to England?" she asked, laughing. "I sold magazine subscriptions by telephone! I worked at it fifteen or thirty minutes at a time and made myself do it every day. I was surprised at how well I did, but it still wasn't enough.

"About four months later, however, someone suggested I might get a newspaper route. I got up at four o'clock every morning and delivered newspapers in the dark, and would you believe I actually enjoyed it? I felt tremendously proud of myself for going to such lengths to achieve my goal. I never dreamed I could be that resourceful and persevering.

"By the time I got to England, I was ready to enjoy every minute of it—and I did!"

Carole, after working every day for a year to fulfill her travel desire of a lifetime, discovered her real payoff came not from the trip, but from her newly earned self-esteem. "I liked myself a lot for earning that trip. I'm making more plans for me, too," she said.

Charlie Shedd, the noted minister, speaker, family counselor, and best-selling author, sometimes surprises his audiences by relating that years ago he promised to give Martha, his wife, fifteen minutes of his time each day. "We don't talk about kids or household or business. We talk about us," he explained.

"People say, what's the use of fifteen minutes? Our fifteen can start at lunch and end at bedtime. The point is, we've agreed to talk once a day. Most couples don't do that.

"We like it. In fact, if I'm out of town, I owe Martha those fifteen minutes a day when I return home."

Whenever our "Time of Your Life" classes consider things they might accomplish fifteen minutes at a time, someone usually echoes Charlie Shedd's sentiments. It's shocking how often our first-place relationships *don't* come first, unless someone decides to make it happen.

What can you do fifteen minutes at a time? Answers to that question range from the sublime (Praise God!) to the ridiculous (clean out the refrigerator). I've profited from many of those creative responses and would love to hear some of your ideas.

A talented caterer said she could prepare to cook a new dish in fifteen minutes. To my look of surprise, she responded: "I'm lazy about researching new recipes. I decided I'd like to add a new dish to my list every week. This way, I could do it."

Men offer a wealth of practical ideas for jobs that can profit from fifteen minutes: post books, sharpen garden tools, shine shoes, learn a new language, listen to Bible tapes, read something pertaining to my job, small household repairs, afternoon nap, hit a few golf balls, research.

Women suggest these: help a child tidy up, make a beautiful dessert, sew a new wardrobe, swim thirty laps, walk, sketch, knit, plan a new schedule, relax, straighten wardrobe closet, plan menus, read books, give myself a facial.

Men and women concentrate hard on discovering ways

116   *Your Magic Fifteen Minutes*

to broaden personal outreach in just fifteen minutes at a time. Here are some good ideas: visit a neighbor, phone an older person, listen to God, share with your child or spouse, spread joy in someone's life, write a note, do something special for each family member.

A career woman with very little personal time in her schedule discovered she could take up piano playing again, by working just fifteen minutes in the morning and fifteen at night. "I'm playing Beethoven pieces now," she announced proudly after a month of her new discipline.

Another woman decided to devote fifteen minutes each evening to begin the next day's housework. She noticed that as she walked through the house retrieving misplaced shoes and watering potted plants, straightening rugs, and plumping cushions, her husband and children followed her lead.

"Each took care of his own stuff without my asking," she marveled. "Now we straighten the house in just a few minutes each night. The kids even lay out their clothes for school the next day."

Even fifteen minutes a day can work magic where full-time living is concerned. Those ideas move life forward. They strengthen my purpose. Most of all, perhaps, they help establish habits of industry.

The Bible has much to say about that, of course. The Book of Proverbs, in particular, encourages us to check our work habits. I like these verses from the Amplified Bible:

> Do you see a man diligent and skillful in his business? He will stand before kings; he will not stand before obscure men.
>
> Proverbs 22:29

The hand of the diligent will rule, but the slothful will be put to forced labor.

Proverbs 12:24

The slothful man will not catch his game, or roast it if he should kill it; but the diligent man will get precious possessions.

Proverbs 12:27

The way of the sluggard is overgrown with thorns [it pricks, lacerates and entangles him], but the way of the righteous is plain and raised like a highway.

Proverbs 15:19

Take fifteen minutes right now and ask yourself these questions:

What is my biggest dream?
How can I make it happen?
What if I worked at this important goal every day for just fifteen minutes?

Try it for a week. You'll be surprised at what God and you can do in just those few minutes!

10

Eight Creative Traits

You can be boundlessly creative.

Full-time living includes one discovery that's pure dynamite: *I am boundlessly creative.*

Since we're modeled after God's image, obviously we inherited a full share of His limitless creative resources. Yet, how much do you know about your special inheritance? Do you think very often about what you really are?

- What, for example, do you like about yourself?
- What do others appreciate about you?
- What are some of the truly unique facets of your special personality?

"There's nothing special about me," one man said flatly, shaking his head. Another joked, "I must have been standing behind the door when talents were passed out. I never had any talent."

Such statements might appear to reflect humility, but think again. Do you believe God left talent and potential out of anyone He created? *Impossible!* If we're made in His image, and if we have the mind of Christ, as the Bible says, it's exciting to imagine the amazing potential God placed in your personality and mine, even before the foundation of the world!

It's our job to seek out our talents, identify them, then foster and encourage the gifts God gave us. As we learn how to do this, we also can improve our ability to perceive and encourage the special traits of our husband or wife, children, and neighbors.

When we begin to see ourselves and others through the eyes of Christ, creative love breaks through. When we focus on what we and others are becoming instead of always putting ourselves down, full-time living takes over.

To do this, I must start with myself. It's time to discover there's a lot more going for me *right now* than I think, and certainly more than I use. It's time to take a hard look at my power to create: I need to take stock of my present assets.

Our "Time of Your Life" workshoppers listed a number of these strengths. They're universal, of course—at least, all of us possess them to some degree—but each can be more fully developed. There's nothing exotic or mysterious here—just good, basic foundation material for full-time living.

It's interesting to rate yourself on our eight creative traits, using Poor, Fair, Average, Good, or Excellent. Remember, however, that this is no test. It's merely an objective assessment of how you see yourself in relation to certain aspects of creativity—each is a trait you can increase.

EIGHT CREATIVE TRAITS

1. VISION: A DESIRE TO MAKE THINGS BETTER. P. T. Barnum said, "If I aim at the sun, I may hit a star." Each of us could decide to aim higher—even aim at the sun!—and

we'd immediately boost our Creativity Quotient.

As J. R. Lowell wrote, "Not failure, but low aim, is a crime."

Brother Andrew, known as "God's Smuggler" to millions throughout the world, quite simply has attempted the impossible throughout his adult life. For three decades he and his confederates have taken the Gospel of Jesus Christ behind the Iron Curtain, risking their lives to do so. Brother Andrew gives God the credit for the success of these daring missions. Recently he told an American congregation, "I'll guarantee that any of you could give out tracts within the Kremlin; that's simple. What's not so simple, however, is to guarantee you'd get out!"

Where did Brother Andrew receive his incredible vision? Would I be willing for God to assign *me* a vision that challenging?

In fact, is my vision anywhere near as large as God would have it be?

Do I pray for Him to increase my imagination, to sanctify it, to make me more daring and less complacent?

Am I even willing to be willing?

As the apostle Paul testified to King Agrippa, "I was not disobedient to the heavenly vision." And as Brother Andrew points out, "God works through people, but He only uses volunteers." Am I ready to volunteer?

PRAYER: *Lord, plant in me the desire to envision Your greatest plan for my life. Amen.*

2. FAITH. With the gift of faith, your creativity flourishes. Jesus said my faith literally could move mountains! Faith gives me the power to push forward toward implementing the big vision God puts in my heart. It pro-

vides the inspiration to begin, the courage to push forward, the determination not to quit.

Why should I *not* have faith in God's purposes concerning me? As the psalmist said, "The Lord will perfect that which concerns me; Your mercy and loving-kindness, O Lord, endure for ever; forsake not the works of Your own hands" (Psalms 138:8 AMPLIFIED).

The apostle Paul wrote:

> And I am convinced and sure of this very thing, that He Who began a good work in you will continue until the day of Jesus Christ—right up to the time of His return—developing [that good work] and perfecting and bringing it to full completion in you.
>
> Philippians 1:6 AMPLIFIED.

Not only is it possible for me to develop a greater faith (not faith in *faith*, I must emphasize, but faith in *God*), but it's absolutely necessary. Faith in God provides me with His boundless creative resources when I need them.

How can I increase my faith? Through prayer, testimony, and above all, through appropriating as total truth, the Word of God. Romans 10:17 says, "So then faith cometh by hearing, and hearing by the word of God" (KJV). Reading the Bible daily increases my faith, hope, and love. God's Word is the basis of all creative thought.

PRAYER: *Father God, make me hungry for Your Word. Amen.*

3. ENTHUSIASM. Dixie Winfrey, an especially talented friend, recalls that when she was a young housewife tied down with three young children, she read this statement: "Success is 80 percent enthusiasm."

If that's true, how successful could you be? What arouses your enthusiasm? Do you enjoy becoming enthusiastic? Dixie did.

"I knew I had very little education or training, or any special talent, but I *did* have enthusiasm," she said. "That one sentence started me on my quest. My natural enthusiasm was the rocket that shot me off the starting pad."

Dixie, once launched, saw her creativity fairly explode in several areas: fashion, merchandising, modeling, lecturing, teaching, catering, and home decoration, to mention a few. She discovered that her creative flair, once aroused, applied to each part of her life.

"I realized I loved to work with women, enjoyed a rapport with women, and loved doing something that added to their life values," she told me. "I wasn't as interested in fashion as I was in helping women help themselves.

"The same art principles hold true in fashion, wardrobe, home decoration, or anything else. One thing stimulated another, for me, and my enthusiasm worked equally well in all areas."

Ralph Waldo Emerson wrote, "Nothing great was ever achieved without enthusiasm. The way of life is wonderful; it is by abandonment."

Your enthusiasm can serve as a catalyst not only for you, but for others. Enthusiasm inspires. It encourages everyone in its path. And no wonder! The word *enthusiasm* comes from the Greek *en theos*, which literally means "God within."

How often do you display this marvelous gift? Remember, increasing your natural enthusiasm inevitably will increase other people's response to you and your ideas.

PRAYER: *Lord, make me properly excited about what You are doing today. Help me exhibit true enthusiasm. Amen.*

4. PERSEVERANCE. Here's a creative trait any of us can develop. As Edward Eggleston said, "Persistent people begin their success where others end in failures."

Jesus told us to persevere. He admonished us to keep on seeking, keep on asking, and keep on knocking. Tremendous, persevering struggle permits the fragile butterfly to break through its fibrous cocoon and fly free. Strong, persistent pecking on its confining shell permits the tiny hummingbird to burst out of its egg and inherit the skies.

Harriet Beecher Stowe said, "When you get into a tight place, and everything goes against you, till it seems as if you could not go on a minute longer, never give up then, for that's just the place and the time that the tide will turn."

Think about the goals and problems in your life today. Are you persevering enough to meet the challenge? Learning how to apply my mind and my energies to the business at hand surely is one of the most creative traits I'll ever master. As E. P. Whipple wrote, "Persistency attracts confidence, more than talents and accomplishments."

The Bible offers total encouragement to those of us who need to learn to persevere. I like the Amplified Bible's beautiful version of Isaiah 40:28–31:

Have you not known? Have you not heard? The everlasting God, the Lord, the Creator of the ends of the earth, does not faint or grow weary; there is no searching of His understanding. He gives power to the faint and weary, and to him who has no might He increases strength—causing it to multiply and making it abound. Even youths shall faint and be weary, and the selected young men shall feebly stumble and fall exhausted. But those who wait for the Lord—who expect, look for and hope in Him—shall change and renew their strength and power; they shall lift their wings and mount up [close to God] as eagles [mount up to the sun]; they shall run and not be weary; they shall walk and not faint or become tired.

I can persevere if I wait upon the Lord, whose strength never can be exhausted. Ask God to increase your power to persist. You can win the prize!

PRAYER: *Lord, teach me not to be a quitter. Thank You that You built into me the power to persevere. Amen.*

5. WILLINGNESS TO PAY THE PRICE. "The world belongs to the energetic," wrote Ralph Waldo Emerson.

Of course we know there's a price to pay, sometimes a big one, if we'd successfully achieve our goals. The question is, am I willing to pay the price?

Joy Ross, a pretty, doll-like dynamo, is one of those housewives who always seems filled with energy and enthusiasm. Joy has the gift of praise. She's also very well organized, with time for an impromptu lunch date with a friend who feels "down," or with her husband Jack, "just because."

Joy invests much time with their son Marcus and daughter Ashley. She also has time for people; time to entertain regularly; time to decorate, maintain, and enjoy their handsome home. Her family's brisk but relaxed life-style seems to welcome creative ideas and offers chances to learn and grow.

"Joy, inside your blond head there's a fantastic executive mind," I declared. "What's your secret? How do you
keep your household humming? How do you keep up with
an ultrasuccessful husband? How do you stay on top of
everything?"

"I do have a wonderful life, and I think it's because my
father taught me to pay the price," Joy said.

"My father has been very successful in business. Very
often I heard him advise young men and women to decide
at the outset how far they're willing to go with their plans
and how much they're willing to pay.

"Dad taught us kids not to start a new project or business
unless it's worth giving five years of hard work to achieve.
That stops most ideas before they get started!

"Marriage is a business, too. A home actually is a small
business, but many people aren't very businesslike at
home. When you get yourself into something, think how
far you plan to take it. Are you willing to pay the price? We
want to become homemakers, but we don't want to scrub
the toilets.

"We want children, but decide to have a baby without
thinking about the eighteen-year commitment to day-in
day-out responsibility.

"We want love, but don't stop to ask ourselves if we'll pay
the price. I decided I'd love deeply, hard, and uncondi-
tionally, and that's a commitment, too."

It's commitment, the decision to pay the price, that
makes Joy's life sing and hum. She seeks God early for
guidance during the day. She cooks a good breakfast for
her husband and children and shows them a happy face.
When they leave the house, Joy immediately attacks the
housework and prepares dinner. "I pay the price early in

the day. From then on I expect good things to happen, and they usually do!" she laughed.

George Washington Carver said, "When you do the common things of life in an uncommon way, you will command the attention of the world." He knew, and Joy Ross knows, the power of total commitment. It's a power that's readily available to each of us. It's still another great creative trait we can get working for us!

Here's how it works. To *commit* means I deliver a person or thing, physically or figuratively, into the charge of another. Imagine, therefore, the power I can release into my life when I deliver that life—every moment and hour of it, every purpose and plan—into God's hands. Dynamite!

Let's agree to commit. Let's decide to pay the price.

PRAYER: *Father, thank You for Jesus, who by His perfect example taught us to pay the price. Please teach me to follow Him. Amen.*

6. PATIENCE TO SOLVE PROBLEMS. "He that can have patience can have what he will," said Benjamin Franklin. Do you recognize the creative power of patience? Have you considered that you could increase your potential by enormous amounts, simply by allowing God to develop mature patience in you?

In fact, according to Thomas A. Edison, patience actually can amount to genius. "Genius is one percent inspiration and ninety-nine percent perspiration," he pronounced. Sometimes our greatest deterrent to acquiring patience is a pride that keeps us from being teachable. As Benjamin Franklin said, "They that will not be counseled cannot be helped."

The problems that force us to exercise patience teach us some of the most creative lessons in life. As the apostle Paul wrote:

> Moreover—let us also be full of joy now! Let us exult and triumph in our troubles and rejoice in our sufferings, knowing that pressure and affliction and hardship produce patient and unswerving endurance. And endurance (fortitude) develops maturity of character—that is, approved faith and tried integrity. And character [of this sort] produces [the habit of] joyful and confident hope of eternal salvation.
>
> Romans 5:3, 4 AMPLIFIED

Perhaps you've seen the gift-shop plaques which read, "Lord make me patient, and do it *right now*." I felt exactly that way about patience until Romans 8:28 at last came alive in my heart: "And we know that all things work together for good to them that love God, to them who are the called according to his purpose" (KJV).

That knowledge, the certainty that I'm one who is called to His purpose, makes patience possible. It turns life into a creative adventure, as I learn how faithful He is to supply the benefits of patience to my striving and impatient life, when I sincerely seek Him.

PRAYER: *Lord, make me willing to become patient. Please help me mature. Amen.*

7. COOPERATION: SUBMISSION TO GOD AND OTHERS. Do you cooperate well? Do you know how to lead? To follow? To be part of a team?

When I learn to cooperate with God and His family, I increase my creative powers past all imagining. After all, can you imagine Barnum without Bailey? Laurel without Hardy? And, seriously, could the Billy Graham evangelistic crusades have been as effective for the Kingdom without the entire team?

A popular song says, "I did it my way." It's not a happy or reassuring song. But what if it said, "I did it His Way?" Imagine *those* lyrics.

The Bible tells us God sets the solitary into families; that it's not good for man to live alone; that if I have aught against my brother, I must go to him and settle it; that in addition to loving the Lord my God with all my heart and mind and soul, I am to love my neighbor as myself.

The Bible has much to say about the creativity of cooperative living. We're told how to achieve life in Christ so that He may dwell in us, and we may learn to walk in the stream of His Spirit.

A living, spirited cooperation with my God should be my highest aim. That really is full-time living! I can think of two saints—David DuPlessis, often called "Mr. Pentecost," and the late Oswald Chambers—who advocate walking so close to God that it's not necessary to pray to know His will, but simply to live in natural cooperation, guided only by checks from His Spirit.

Oswald Chambers wrote in *My Utmost for His Highest*:

> To be so much in contact with God that you never need to ask Him to show you His will, is to be nearing the final stage of your discipline in the life of faith.
>
> When you are rightly related to God, it is a life

of freedom and liberty and delight, you *are* God's
will, and all your common-sense decisions are His
will for you unless He checks. You decide things
in perfect delightful friendship with God, knowing that if your decisions are wrong He will always
check; when He checks, stop at once.

What a magnificent goal, that sort of cooperation! And
if I should learn to cooperate and submit to God, obviously
He gives me the same creative power within the Body of
Christ. As Peter wrote in 1 Peter 5:5–7 KJV:

> . . . all of you be subject one to another, and
> be clothed with humility: for God resisteth the
> proud, and giveth grace to the humble. Humble
> yourselves therefore under the mighty hand of
> God, that he may exalt you in due time: Casting
> all your care upon him; for he careth for you.

The creative trait of cooperation requires us to learn
humility. As the evangelist Dwight L. Moody said, "Be
humble or you'll stumble."

But Phillips Brooks, the great New England minister of
the nineteenth century, said, "The true way to be humble
is not to stoop till thou art smaller than thyself, but to stand
at thy real height against some higher nature that shall
show thee what the real smallness of thy greatest greatness
is."

John Donne wrote, "No man is an island." Full-time living requires the creative and inspired use of my cooperation in ever-increasing ways. As Phillips Brooks also
pointed out, "No grace or blessing is truly ours until we are

aware that God has blessed someone else with it through us."

PRAYER: *Father, please teach me to live and work with You and Yours. Teach me to cooperate. Amen.*

8. WISDOM. Am I wise? W. L. Phelps said, "At a certain age some people 's minds close up; they live on their intellectual fat."

The Bible tells us Jesus increased in wisdom and stature, and it tells us we are supposed to do the same. There's no cut-off point in my life, as far as acquiring wisdom is concerned. The Bible exhorts me to seek diligently after God's wisdom, which is the mind of Christ.

How do I do that?

The creative trait of wisdom is one you and I can increase dramatically, beginning today. As we're told in James 1:5–8 (KJV), we can receive every bit of the wisdom we need for full-time living, when we meet God's stipulations.

> If any of you lack wisdom, let him ask of God, that giveth to all men liberally, and upbraideth not; and it shall be given him. But let him ask in faith, nothing wavering. For he that wavereth is like a wave of the sea driven with the wind and tossed. For let not that man think that he shall receive any thing of the Lord. A double minded man is unstable in all his ways.

The priceless gift of wisdom, according to the Bible, remains readily available to me. The Bible abounds in instructions toward wisdom. The Book of Proverbs, in particular, points us to the wisdom of God. The businessman, student, career woman, parent, or housewife who would like to program his or her mind with real precepts of success would be well advised to read one of the thirty-one rich chapters of Proverbs each day of the month.

We can become rich in wisdom. Solomon prayed for wisdom, and so should we. God wants to provide it for us.

PRAYER: *Father God, help me to pray wisely. Let me seek the mind of Christ and ask each day for Your deepest wisdom. Thank You. Amen.*

These are the eight creative traits you can appropriate for your life, with God's help. Ask Him to give you vision, faith, enthusiasm, perseverance, a willingness to pay the price, patience, cooperation, and wisdom.

These are not talents, but gifts. God says they are yours for the asking. Let's begin to ask!

11

Overcoming Fear and Failure

*Failure can change to victory
in your life.*

It's entirely possible for us to overcome our lifetime habits of fear and failure. As you know, we'll always encounter traps, pitfalls, and tricks of Satan. None of us will discover an *easy* road to full-time living.

Nevertheless, we can learn to throw off the baleful influences of former mind and habit sets. We can learn to recognize danger signals and divert them.

How? The Bible has many answers. Romans 12:2 says, "And be not conformed to this world: but be ye transformed by the renewing of your mind, that ye may prove what is that good, and acceptable, and perfect, will of God" (KJV).

James 4:7 instructs us, ". . . Resist the devil, and he will flee from you" (KJV).

Fear can manifest itself so subtly that we don't even recognize it. Fear masks itself in numerous ways; it hides, deceives, and dissembles so cleverly that it's hard to identify as the sin behind what seems to be quite another problem.

137

Lori, for example, felt puzzled as to why she'd soured her whole week by putting off making two telephone calls. "I just dawdled around, putting them off from day to day, which somehow prevented me from doing my other work as well as usual," she confessed. "Why did I procrastinate and let those phone calls make me miserable?"

She had no idea. However, when she thought further, Lori realized she'd had "a tad of fear" about phoning.

"That's dumb, though," she said with a frown. "I had to ask two women I don't know to help with a school program, and I knew they wouldn't want to do it. I guess I felt I couldn't cope with two turndowns right now, so I procrastinated. Then I despised myself for doing it. Two little phone calls robbed me of my joy!"

Lori learned something new about herself that day. "I guess the little fears we don't express add up to depression," she summed up. "From now on, whenever I'm slow to act, I plan to ask myself why."

The "something" that slows us down often can be traced to fear or anxiety buried below the conscious level. The good news is, such vague but unsettling feelings don't need to deter us further. I can overcome fear! In Isaiah 41:13, there's a wonderful promise: "For I the Lord thy God will hold thy right hand, saying unto thee, Fear not; I will help thee" (KJV).

Here are some ways to overcome fear:

1. Determine what it is you are afraid of. Pinpoint it. Examine it. Look at it for exactly what it is. Discover exactly what you must deal with.

2. Discover your reasons for being afraid of this or that. Ask for God's wisdom to help you see exactly when and

where this fear or inhibition started. If you're not certain you know the reason or reasons, then get expert counseling.

3. Get your fear out in the open. Drag it out where you can attack it. Often a surprisingly small thing has tried to frighten you.

4. Fill your mind full of faith facts. Fear and faith cannot coexist. Your mind must choose one or the other. The Bible tells you that God is not the author of fear, so you don't have to accept unreasonable fear. You will choose faith.

5. Do your best. Decide to leave all results to the Lord. After all, "If God be for us, who can be against us?"

6. Learn to stand up to your fear and dare it to do its worst. Actually, most fear springs from your own imagination. As Mark Twain said, "I'm an old man and have known many troubles, but most of them never happened."

7. Sometimes your fear is based on fact. When that happens, you can overcome. God will help you release the spiritual and mental strength you need. "Yea, though I walk through the valley of the shadow of death, I will fear no evil: for thou art with me; thy rod and thy staff they comfort me" (Psalms 23:4 KJV). The word *comfort* means "with strength." Pray! Praise! And God will replace your fear with supernatural strength.

When I take dominion over my life—mind, body, and spirit—I can decide to weed out those things which are detrimental to my best interests. I can take charge of myself. I can decide to quit losing and start winning, for a change.

However, I'd better be prepared for the excuses I'll

throw at myself—sometimes the very flimsiest of reasons for not changing, or alibis as to why I'd better not try. It's important that I shoot straight with myself here; it's time to admit that excuses and alibis add up to failure, and I don't want to fail! Here are some common reasons why people fail:

1. UNWILLINGNESS TO CHANGE. "If I quit smoking I'll gain weight. I'd better lose ten pounds first," one man said. Who is he kidding?

My friend Sheila says she drinks too much coffee, so she asked a prayer friend to pray she'd break the habit. "Sheila, do you really want to stop drinking coffee?" the friend asked.

"No, I don't!" Sheila said, surprised.

"That's your answer," her friend told her. "When you decide to stop drinking coffee, God will help you!"

2. PROCRASTINATION. Have you noticed that when you or I need to lose weight, we always mean to begin our diet next Monday? Whenever something needs doing, especially when it's hard to begin, I need to ask myself: Why not today? As G. H. Lorimer said, "Putting off an easy thing makes it hard, and putting off a hard one makes it impossible."

Getting the hate-to-do-it items started now releases in me a wellspring of energy which produces a winning attitude. Procrastination is a failure trait.

3. INABILITY TO TRY NEW THINGS. When is the last time you tried something new? Think. For some of us, the realization is painful; we really don't want to do, see, taste, or feel anything with which we aren't familiar.

However, insistence on things remaining the same

guarantees failure. Life changes, moves, grows continually. Unless I allow my life to flow, it must stagnate.

We all know people who can't or won't try new things—even a new route to work, a new hairdo, or a different flavor of ice cream. How about me? Am I open to suggestions?

4. I'M TOO YOUNG (TOO OLD). The *young* failure always is waiting to become two, five, or ten years older, while the *old* failure says he or she should have started ten, fifteen, or twenty years ago.

Actually, the day God gives me the go-ahead is the right day to begin, regardless of my age. Chronological age has little to do with most decisions a healthy person makes.

Moses started leading his people toward the Promised Land when he was eighty years old. By contrast, Mozart wrote some important compositions, many of them enormously complex, while still a youth. Nobody told the child prodigy he was "too young" to compose. I enjoy collecting stories about people who refuse to believe they're too old. Here are some of my favorites.

- One of the most popular classes at the Parkwood Nursing Home in Chattanooga, Tennessee, is belly dancing. The average age of the students there is 90. The oldest is 101.
- Conductor Leopold Stokowski has signed a new five-year recording contract. He's ninety-five years old.
- Francis Xavier Cross of the Lady of Victory Church, Washington, D. C., is America's oldest altar boy. He's ninety years old and has been attending church daily since 1896.
- Rita Reutter was elected "homecoming" queen at

Florida Tech in Orlando. Rita is a fifty-eight-year-old
grandmother studying guidance counseling.
• Samuel Matkoff astonished nurses at Long Beach
Hospital in California by doing the hustle and the
fox-trot. He's 101.
• Jeannette Smith of Mumbles, Wales, has just opened a
savings account "for her old age." Jeannette is 107!

The question is, what has God planned for me today?
"Too young" and "too old" really don't exist.

5. NOT ENOUGH MONEY. Ultimately that can't possibly be
true, if my Father owns the cattle on a thousand hills.
There's always plenty of money to finance God's plans.
The faith-filled Christian learns not to allow any sort of
lack to slow him down, much less to halt God's work in his
life.

Not enough money? Never. Jesus told us to ask God to
supply our needs. He said we are to worry about nothing.
He told us we have not because we ask not.

As Corrie ten Boom wrote, "My father always provided
the ticket just when I needed it—just before I boarded the
train." When I believe my needs will be supplied, my plans
work out. If I convince myself there won't be enough capi-
tal, inevitably there's failure ahead.

6. FEAR OF CRITICISM. "Go home and believe in your-
selves more," Phillips Brooks told his congregation. That's
good advice, because the individual who looks over his
shoulder in fear of possible criticism actually is aiding and
abetting the enemy—failure.

I need to decide to do my best and allow God to handle
the outcome. I must learn to become a God pleaser instead
of a man pleaser. As Horace Mann wrote, "Character is

what God and the angels know of us; reputation is what men and women think of us."

Whom do I really want to please? Why should I allow possible future criticism to decide my course of action?

7. NOT ENOUGH TIME. Someone has said it's not the things we do that we regret, but the things we don't do. Have I developed the habit of turning down opportunities because I think I have too little time? That's a failure trait.

Once, at a key moment in my life, I nearly did just that. An editor telephoned to ask me to consider writing a book. I replied that I couldn't possibly write a book; I'd never written one before, and I had no time to learn how since I had a full-time job in addition to my duties as wife, mother, and housewife. How could I take on another thing?

"Don't give me an answer today," he replied. "Pray about it and I'll telephone on Friday, after you decide."

When I prayed, the Lord showed me how I could schedule my meager time and could, with stringent effort, produce the book—if nothing happened to intervene. When I gave the editor my answer, he said, "Fine. If you're willing to trust God, then so am I!"

That book got none of my best time or energies. Most of the writing was done at night, between ten and two o'clock. Needless to say, I was tired, but somehow it got written— and that book opened the door to all the other beautiful writing opportunities I've enjoyed since then.

How often I wonder, what if I really had decided I didn't have time to write that book? I learned from that episode to seek God before I decide I don't have enough time. I must let Him provide the wisdom I need!

Knowing these and other causes of our fears and failures can help us fight off Satan's attacks on our ideas and plans. It's important for me to examine whatever fact, idea, or misconception might hinder the will of God for my life.

I can learn to overcome fear. I don't have to live as a failure. Most assuredly, the Bible tells me I'm designed for full-time living!

12

The Best Time

*Catching the vision
of what you can be.*

"Had lunch with ol' Joe," Al told me. "I guess they're in bad shape at their house." I handed Al a cup of coffee as he continued, "The poor guy is having it tough. He lost a big case [Joe is a lawyer] and probably has too much money tied up in investments, so money's tight.

"He's scared they'll have to take the kids out of private school. She says if he does, she'll leave him. She's insisting they buy that beach condominium *now,* and he says there's no way.

"Things are so bad at home, Joe can't get a grip on his business or himself. He says they have no communication. She gives him no encouragement. The guy looks beat, and he admits he almost wishes she *would* leave him."

Al sipped his coffee in silence for a moment, then gave one last comment. "I wish someone would tell Helen what Jackie Dark told you. It might save that marriage."

I thought back to a night baseball game in Oakland, California, which Al and I, newly married, attended with the beautiful red-haired wife of then Oakland Athletics manager Alvin Dark. Between Jackie's enthusiastic yells for the A's, we enjoyed an equally spirited evening of sharing the Lord. Sometime during all that action, Jackie said something which excited me tremendously.

"I wish every Christian wife in America would decide to pray for her husband every hour of the day. Imagine what strong Christian men God could raise up in this country! Imagine what kind of homes we'd have!"

My imagination caught fire. "Oh, Jackie, do you pray for Alvin every hour?" I exclaimed.

"No," she answered honestly, "lots of times I forget. But I'm trying, because I know I have a great part to play in his becoming what God intends him to be."

"Doesn't that take a lot of time?"

"Not really. Anyhow, I've got nothing more important to do with my time," she answered quietly. "After all, I'm the only woman in the world privileged to fill that job." Then and there I decided to try Jackie's idea. That decision has had great impact on our lives and in our home, despite the fact that I, like Jackie, still don't ever bat a thousand!

Even so, Al and I keep track of each other's business and social calendars. Whenever he makes a scheduled call on a client, he knows I'm praying for them. If I lunch with friends, I know Al will pray that we're having fun and that the Lord will be present. Al depends on me to pray for his clients and business dealings; I depend on him to pray for each seminar and each book chapter. It's neat!

The point is, this habit saves us a tremendous number of false steps and much unnecessary doubt. It's great to receive such silent encouragement. It's beautiful to know

God's arms link my husband and me as we work clear across town from one another.

"Marriage is so daily," an older woman murmured to her companion. She's right, but through prayer even mundane activities become purposeful and interesting. Also, when one person boosts another, both are strengthened.

The husband and wife who are united *spiritually*—as opposed to just physically, intellectually, financially, as parents, citizens, and so forth—inevitably exhibit some of the most strongly successful lives you'll meet.

Where Christ is the Cornerstone, God invariably turns marriage into a special creativity center. These days more and more couples are discovering fantastic facts about full-time living as they seek God's plan for their families.

You probably know people who, after years of secular marriage, discovered holy matrimony. Perhaps that's happening to you. I can think of one couple, a minister and his gifted wife, who actually separated for eighteen months and started over—visiting, courting, talking, confronting, learning to pray aloud together, dating, seeking God's will for their relationship—before they remarried. That's an extreme case. Nevertheless, this couple, with God's help, built a dynamic new relationship.

Full-time living results from God's guiding two quite ordinary people into extraordinary new lives. Al and I discovered this five years ago, as we prayed about whether or not we should marry. Is it possible to marry—*really* marry—after experiencing socially acceptable but godless marriages which ended in divorce? Could God still teach us anything? Were we too old to change?

From the many excellent books concerning Christian

marriage, Al and I chose the Holy Bible. Using a concordance, we studied such topics as *marriage, husband, wife, man, woman,* and so on, and began to thrill to the possibilities of a new and guaranteed successful way of life. We sensed that God had much more for us than we'd dreamed, and He did!

Where two people agree to abandon sin, selfishness, failure traits, fears, and laziness in exchange for the real promise of abundant life, God can and will meet them at their point of need. Bad, lackluster, or even desperate marriages can be transformed where husband and wife allow God to work. If I need a miracle, I should ask for it! If I'm married to someone who is impossible, I can try praying for him or her once an hour for a month. Anything might happen!

Take another look at our eight creative traits in chapter ten, and you'll think of individuals or couples who mirror them. In our case, Billy and Edith Beers come to mind.

The Beers offered to give Al and me a wedding party. What a beautiful gift, but since it was a very quiet second wedding, I declined. Edith insisted. "I want you to have something very special to remember," she told me. "I didn't think I wanted a reception when Billy and I married, but his sister and our children honored us anyhow, and it had so much meaning that I decided someday I'd pass it on."

It must have been as beautiful as that wedding feast where Jesus turned water into wine. He came to our feast too, that beautiful Easter afternoon—Resurrection Sunday—in Billy's and Edith's exquisite tiered garden. Dogwoods in full bloom, masses of azaleas and potted lilies, echoed our gladness. A young Episcopal priest played the guitar as everyone sang "Amazing Grace" and "He's Got the Whole World in His Hands." Our joy exploded.

But Billy and Edith gave us so much more than a party: They gave us an important understanding of unstinting hospitality. God chose those two exceptionally creative servants to demonstrate how lavish, openhanded, and even extravagant Christian love can be, on occasion.

They're still teaching us. Supposedly retired, Billy spends hours each week ministering to alcoholics. Edith recently gave an elaborate Christmas luncheon for numerous elderly ladies. "These are friends of my mother, or neighbors, or women recently widowed," Edith said. "They might not bother with a Christmas tree or lights or music, so they can share ours." When I exclaimed at her thoughtfulness, Edith blushed. "It gives me pleasure," she said. "Besides, I'll be old, too, someday."

Billy and Edith Beers demonstrate the beautiful balance that's built into the full-time living God created us to experience. There's time, plenty of time, for everything He calls me to do. There's time for joy, for giving, for new depths of experience. There's time for growth, renewal, and healing; time to discover fresh wellsprings of the tough and enduring love each of us needs.

Throughout this book, I've challenged you to discover ways by which you can increase your output, or your leisure and personal time, by at least 100 percent. Some of us can expand our lives even more than that.

Strong, workable marriages encourage such expansion. Why don't we celebrate those marriages which thrive? I believe God does! I'd like to share four stories involving couples who allowed God to change them—sometimes radically—into unique and inspiring personalities. Each knows much about full-time living, yet any of these eight people probably would describe himself as "ordinary" or "average." You decide for yourself.

Let's begin with Lee Watson and his wife, Lois, from Atlanta, Georgia. Lee, who grew up in the northern Georgia mountains during the Depression, became a Christian at age eighteen "because Lois wouldn't have me unless I did."

"I had a fifth-grade education, and I felt my inabilities," Lee told me. "There weren't a lot of jobs I could get, but I became a baker, and Lois and I did all right.

"Those days, I saw people living for the devil and prospering like mad. Psalm Thirty-Seven says, though, 'A little that a righteous man hath is better than the riches of many wicked.' Then one day another Scripture hit me: 'Seek ye first the kingdom of God and His righteousness, and all these things shall be added unto you.'

"I wasn't really a witness for the Lord. But then I started praying a prayer that went on for years, that God would let me retire at fifty and I'd work full-time for Him the rest of my life. One day I told God, 'I'll go where You want me to go, do what You want me to do, and say what You want me to say.' I had no idea what I really was praying, though I thought I did."

Before Lee Watson turned fifty, the Lord took him up on his offer. Lee and Lois sold some property they owned and received a handsome profit. At the height of his earning powers, Lee Watson kept his promise to God. He retired. He and Lois built a multi-unit apartment house to provide income so they can work full-time for Jesus.

What has happened in the twenty years since? "I've

traveled in about twenty foreign countries and all over the United States for the Gospel's sake," Lee told me. He has had many surprising experiences. He recalled traveling to Alaska and wading through six-foot snowdrifts to speak to congregations as small as fifteen worshipers.

"Lord, why am I here?" he prayed silently. Soon he knew. "Three people received Christ and six others were filled with the Holy Ghost that day," he said. "I'd go anywhere for that."

Lee and Lois, who exemplify full-time living, say, "The Lord will answer your prayer if you're sincere. The whole thing is obedience."

"However," Lee cautioned, "don't tell Him you'll go where He wants you to go and do what He wants you to do unless you really mean it. God will take you up on that!"

Nancy Pafford, a College Park, Georgia, housewife in her late thirties, says her husband Johnny encouraged her to take the steps which brought some surprising changes to their household.

As a teenager, Nancy quit school to get married, had three children, then an early divorce. "I had to work, but had no qualifications," Nancy told me. "I lied my way into several good jobs. When they asked if I'd finished high school I'd say 'of course,' and nobody ever checked me out.

"When Johnny and I married three years ago, I decided I must return to school and get my diploma. By this time I had a very low self-opinion, and in fact was so ashamed of my lack of education that I'd never admitted to my kids that their mother was a dropout.

"When I decided to return to high school, I was so afraid of failure I didn't tell my kids or even my parents about my plans—only Johnny. He said, 'Fantastic!' He was overjoyed that I wanted to do it and had the confidence to do it. He predicted I'd even go on to college."

Nancy attended school in the daytime so her children wouldn't suspect, in case she failed. Her teachers assured her she'd pass, and that she'd go on to college. "I didn't believe them," Nancy said. "I thought they were psyching me up. When my final scores arrived in the mail just before Christmas, they were quite high. I had to read the letter three times before I could accept it!

"Those scores broke my mental block. They gave me an ardent desire to go to college."

Nancy, still timid about her success, decided to tell her children one at a time. "I thought I was really open to ridicule," she explained. "I didn't know what they'd say."

Christopher, the oldest, blurted out, "I'm so proud of my mom! If you're going to college, wait for me. I'll go anywhere you want to go." Teicher, Nancy's fifteen-year-old daughter, reacted differently. "I've known it all along," she said. "I didn't know what you were doing, but there was a big change in you, and I could feel it." Teicher declared the whole household changed as Nancy's attitudes began to change. Dino, eleven, just grinned and teased his mom, but Nancy could tell he was pleased.

What's next for Johnny and Nancy? She'll enter college next fall, headed for a degree in psychology. "Johnny and I have kept foster children in our home for the past three years. Some are emotionally disturbed, so I need professional training," she explained. "I want to become a guidance counselor. The other day a professional with one of our state agencies asked me to apply for a job with them after I've completed two years of college work.

"Life really is opening up for us."

I heard David Vick's testimony on a Christian network television program. Impressed by the intensity of his commitment as a businessman, I promptly telephoned David at his home in Argyle, Texas, where he and Joanne work and rear their family.

David is a craftsman. Three years ago, as he tried out a router his mother gave him for his birthday, he became inspired to create some wooden plaques. These turned out to be popular gift items. A friend suggested he try placing a few in Christian bookstores, and that was the beginning!

"I had no intention of starting a business," David told me. "However, God led Joanne and me one step at a time, until today we have a nationwide business called Faith Creations, Incorporated. It includes not only our work, but that of other Christian craftsmen who produce art items for homes and offices. This past Christmas we had twenty-five people working for us."

The part-time venture David started three years ago with just one hundred dollars initial outlay, this year anticipates a sales total of more than one million dollars. "I see Faith Creations as a continuing venture that will get bigger and bigger as God leads," David told me.

"The Lord often speaks to me through my wife. Joanne has much spiritual discernment, and she helps me make decisions. She also helps with design work and attends sales conferences.

"I believe where a man and woman pray together for God's vision, you don't need amazing talent or know-how. He'll take what you've got and do great things, when you put Him first.

"We don't have any special success secret of our own, but we believe the admonition found in James 1:5 that says, 'If any of you lack wisdom let him ask of the Lord who gives to all men liberally . . . .' "

There's much more to the story of this talented couple, but that's for David and Joanne Vick to tell. What comes through to an outsider, though, is David's belief that there's unlimited creativity available to the husband and wife who seek Christ's way of life.

The only thing deceptive about Joe and Sara Edwards of Saint Simons Island, Georgia, is their looks. It's hard to imagine this youthful, smiling couple to be parents of five grown or nearly grown sons and daughters and the grandparents of a toddler. Beyond that, Joe Edwards seems far too young to have built a neighborhood bakery into a prosperous pie company that sells in thirty-eight states.

"We started early," Sara says with a smile. "Joe was twenty and I was seventeen when we married. We were very much in love and didn't have much money, so were glad to move in with Joe's dad in exchange for my keeping house.

"My father died when I was seven, and I had no brothers, so I didn't know anything about men. I also didn't know how to keep house or cook. Now I was keeping house for three men—Joe's dad, Joe, and his brother.

"I had to learn by pitching in and doing it, which might be the best way. We had five children in seven years, so with Joe working long hours at the bakery, I had to learn to be orderly and plan my days. With a large family, you must learn to plan, or else live in a state of confusion.

"By then I thought I had everything my heart desired: a wonderful husband, beautiful children, a lovely home, my health, and Joe and the children healthy and well adjusted. Still there was something missing in my life. I lacked a peace and had little confidence in myself and my abilities. I set high standards for myself, standards I couldn't attain. I wanted to be a perfect wife and mother. I looked at other people's lives and realized the blessings in mine and felt all the more guilty for not being content.

"When I was twenty-nine and Joe thirty-two we both invited Christ into our lives as a personal Saviour. Joshua 24:15 (KJV) came to be the basis of our home: ". . . as for me and my house, we will serve the Lord." The emptiness was now filled by peace. Accepting Jesus Christ into our lives made a good marriage even better. We turned every detail over to Jesus, from ourselves, our home, our children, our business and all our time and energy.

"Building a home is my career and as the Bible says, Except the Lord builds the house, they labour in vain that build it . . . (Psalms 127:1 KJV). Building takes planning, time, energy, and enthusiasm. Loving your husband and children and showing your love to them also takes planning, time, energy, and enthusiasm. Planning special surprises for the family is a joy for me. One night I fixed a Chinese dinner for them, served it on a make-do table, and we sat on the floor to dine. Or sometimes we had picnic dinners in our woods. I love to send or tuck an "I love you" note in an unexpected place and put special things in their rooms such as a flower or a pack of gum.

"For twenty-two years Joe and I have walked together, worked together, and shared common goals. As Amos 3:3 (KJV) says, 'Can two walk together, except they be agreed?'

God is now teaching us to plan together and share the desires of our hearts with each other.

"Several years ago, we took off two months to realign our lives. Joe and I spent time together, walked the beach, shared, and let the Lord redirect us. We write out our priorities, plans, and our goals and take a fresh look at them often. We go aside regularly to pray about our family and personal goals. A marriage builds when you share your point of view and discuss things until you understand each other. Communication is such a key to your relationship with God, your husband and family. Joe and I have found it so helpful to spend time together and write our goals, because if you have no target, your aim has no direction. We know our plans and our goals are heading in the direction to achieve and win as is expressed in Philippians 3:13, 14.

Ordinary stories about ordinary people? Perhaps. But they illustrate how the rest of us can possess that extraordinary vision and sensitivity to God's will, the unusual purpose, the rare willingness to set goals and work hard.

These are Christians whose devotion to the Kingdom of God and His righteousness bring forth that precious byproduct called full-time living.

These are men and women like you and me. Like you and me, they hold the keys to the Kingdom.

As Jesus said, "The kingdom of heaven is within you."

But what about you? What about me? Where will God take us? What will our lives stand for? What is His plan for our lives? I believe we'll find the answer to those questions in the final verse of the Book of John:

And there are also many other things which Jesus did, the which, if they should be written every one, I suppose that even the world itself could not contain the books that should be written. Amen.

John 21:25 KJV

As for our future, perhaps we sing about it when we sing verse four of "Amazing Grace":

When we've been there ten thousand years,
Bright shining as the sun,
We've no less days to sing God's praise,
Than when we'd first begun.